WILD OATS

A ROMANCE OF THE OLD WEST
BY JAMES McLURE

★

★

DRAMATISTS
PLAY SERVICE
INC.

WILD OATS was presented by the Center Theater Group at the Mark Taper Forum, in Los Angeles, on June 16, 1984. It was directed by Tom Moore; the set design was by Ralph Funicello; the costumes were by Robert Blackman; the lighting was by Martin Aronstein; and the music was composed, adapted and arranged by Larry Delinger. The cast was as follows:

PIANO PLAYER	Robert Webb
GUITAR/BANJO PLAYER	Sean Michael Kelly
SOUND MAN	David L. Krebs
BARTENDER	Douglas Blair
DRUNK	Timothy Donoghue
MADAM	Constance Ball
BARGIRL	Jenna Cole
COWBOY	Stephen Roberts
GAMBLER	Robert Yacko
LIBERTY	Michael Richards
WILSON	Charles Gregory
ANGEL EYES	John Wesley
COLONEL CROFTUS THUNDER	Ken Ruta
CORPORAL CROW	Howland Chamberlin
KATE THUNDER	Debora May
HARRY THUNDER	Mark Blum
MUZ	Thomas Oglesby
JACK ROVER	Mark Harelick
INNKEEPER'S DAUGHTER	Jenna Cole
IKE GAMMON	Fred Applegate
SIM GAMMON	Gary Dontzig
JANE GAMMON	Cynthia Darlow
SENOR MORALES	Tom Rosqui
SHERIFF	David Sage
MR. KLIEGLE	John Randolph
MR. LEKO	Ralph Drischell
AMELIA DOLORES MORALES	Eve Roberts
BEAR	Robert Yacko
MARSHAL	Stephen Roberts

AUTHOR'S NOTE

WILD OATS is an affectionate tribute to the men and women of the late 19th century who toured the American West as travelling players. Accordingly, the play can be performed with a minimum of theatrical effects—i.e., lighting, set, costumes, since the essence of touring theatricals has always been "a board, a passion and a tatter." It was not unusual for companies of that era, touring the Old West, to perform Shakespeare with less than ten players through the ingenuity of double, triple, quadruple casting—in fact, I think this is half the fun.

WILD OATS

ACT ONE

SCENE 1

The Last Chance Saloon.
A saloon in the Old West of the 1880's, assorted cowpokes, old geezers, a piano player, and dance hall girls of dubious moral virtue. The piano player tinkles out a low-key version of "I Dream Of Jeannie." The rustic mood of pastoral prairie is rudely broken by the intrusion of three brutish-looking gunfighters.
A brief barroom brawl breaks out and in a flurry of motion, during which the piano player shifts to a spirited version of "Tavern in the Town," the bar is vacated by the townspeople as the gunfighters abscond with liquor and money from the cash box.
Suddenly, we hear a thunder of hooves. The piano player skips into playing "Gary Owen"—the anthem of the Seventh Cavalry. *

THUNDER. (*Offstage.*) CHAARRRGE! (*Enter Colonel Croftus Thunder and Corporal Fernando O'Fienne Crow. They enter, sabre and tomahawk drawn, in a cloud of dust.*) Seventh Cavalry, column halt!
CROW. Aye, aye, Colonel Thunder. (*He stops. Crow runs into him. They observe the situation.*)
THUNDER. (*Dejectedly.*) Once again, Corporal Crow, the Cavalry seems to be too late to save the day.
CROW. Colonel, darlin', we don't have to save the day. We're retired, remember?
THUNDER. True, Crow, my faithful Irish-Indian companion and trusted Army Scout.
CROW. Retired.
THUNDER. Retired. From the Glorious Seventh Cavalry. (*The piano player plays* "Gary Owen.") Well, let's have a drink. My gullet's as parched as a prickley pear.

CROW. A drink, sir?

THUNDER. We've been a-ridin' the range, a-ridin' the purple sage, in search of deserters from the Glorious Seventh Cavalry. (*Piano—*"Gary Owen.") A-ridin' the range ... a-ridin' the range ... A-RIDIN' THE RANGE, through heat, through sun, through sand, and all in a state of total sobriety. Worst afternoon of my life. (*He pounds the bar. A frightened bartender pops up.*) Whiskey and make it Irish.

BARTENDER. We don't serve Indians here.

THUNDER. Good, I don't want any! (*The Bartender serves the drinks.*) To the Glorious Seventh Cavalry! (*The piano player plays* "Gary Owen.")

CROW. Colonel, darlin', one question.

THUNDER. Speak, Crow, my faithful Irish-Indian companion and trusted Army scout.

CROW. What in bejesus' name are we doin' here?

THUNDER. Doin' here? Why we're ridin' the range. Ridin' the range through heat, through sun—

CROW. Yes, Colonel, but *why* are we ridin' the range?

THUNDER. We do it out of duty. A sense of duty to the glorious ...

CROW. A sense of duty? Or is it—dare I say it—could it be—a sense of guilt?

THUNDER. (*Enormous guilt.*) Guilt?

CROW. Yes, guilt. You know of whom I speak, sir.

THUNDER. Speak no more of her.

CROW. I speak of one Miss Amelia, that damaged dandelion of the prairie whom you deceived years ago with a false marriage, passing yourself off as a certain Captain Seymour. Then leaving her behind to break her heart, and you since marrying another woman and having a son by her to boot. Oh, the shame.

THUNDER. Why, oh, why did I persist in sowing my wild oats? And Amelia, the only woman I ever truly loved.

CROW. Aye, sir, and now she's dead. Another judgement on yourself. And now you've a son at West Point whom you seldom see out of guilt, and whom I—out of a string of amazing coincidences—have never seen. All because of you and your wild oats.

THUNDER. Speak no more to me of my wild oats.

CROW. Wild oats!

THUNDER. Why, oh why, must you torment me with my wild oats? *You*, who arranged to procure the mock clergyman that performed the sham marriage that led to the deceitful deception, that resulted in the dire predicament, which developed into the years of yearning for the aforementioned, much-suffering, nearly-forgotten Miss Amelia, my wife, my former bride. Ah well, ah well—and it's all your fault!

CROW. True, I arranged the mock marriage with the miscreant minister which led to the contumely connubials, which dragged you down the road to deceit and temptation, which is just at the cross roads of moral guilt and obligation, just south of Amarillo. In short, you had to vamoose before the jig was up. And I have to share the blame. And if you can follow all of that, you're a better man than I. (*Aside.*) Actually, the minister I hired was a bonafide clergyman. And so the Colonel was actually legally married—My plan was to bring the two love birds together. My plan was for the Colonel to be forced to stay with Amelia and never leave. It was a foolproof plan.

THUNDER. How many years has it been since I left Amelia?

CROW. Thirty. (*Aside.*) Actually, no plan is foolproof.

THUNDER. And so we ended up spending our lives in service of the glorious Seventh Cavalry! (*The piano player plays* "Gary Owen," *and segues into* "We Shall Gather at the River."* *Ephraim Smooth, a minister, enters. All in black, ferret-faced, pale. From the side he represents a balding spider, an effect he tries to counterbalance with a sickening display of benevolence.*)

EPHRAIM. Ah, visitors! Travellers! Weary wayfarers on the wicked road of life. You've come to the right place. For spiritual comfort, guidance and rest this is the only port in a storm.

THUNDER. It's also the only saloon in town.

EPHRAIM. Presently a saloon, soon to be a tabernacle of hope and revival. Hallelujah! Praise the Lord.

CROW. And pass the plate.

EPHRAIM. Are you a Christian?

CROW. No, sorry, I'm Catholic.

EPHRAIM. But do you have the spirit?

---

*See Special Note on copyright page.

CROW. Oh, if it's spirits you mean—the Colonel's your man!

THUNDER. Cheers!

CROW. Cheers!

THUNDER. Say, tell me, what's a preacher doing in a red-eye parlor?

EPHRAIM. I am Ephraim Smooth, pastor of the Church of Christian Suffering and Denial, and the executor of the estate of a lady richly left. This saloon happens to be one of her holdings. When the will of her late father becomes final I—that is, *she*—will become the richest person in the territory, inheriting the lands of the late Loftus Thunder.

CROW. Loftus Thunder!

THUNDER. Loftus Thunder!?

EPHRAIM. You heard me. Loftus Thunder.

THUNDER. Loftus Thunder! My second cousin—dead?

EPHRAIM. As a doornail.

THUNDER. Actually, second cousin twice removed. Once by marriage, once on general principles.

EPHRAIM. True, he led a wild, sinful life. Wine, women, song, women, women, women—

THUNDER. Loftus always recognized his priorities.

EPHRAIM. But before he died I converted him to religion. He died reborn! Out of gratitude he made me executor of his estate. Soon I will control—that is, *advise* his daughter Kate Thunder.

THUNDER. My niece Kate. As pretty a little thing as ever you saw. Tender like a flower, delicate as a bud. (*Offstage Kate yelling.*)

KATE. Where the hell is everybody? (*Kate Thunder stomps in. She wears a long black dress with a high starched collar, cowboy boots under her dress.*)

KATE. Uncle Croftus!

THUNDER. Mary Kate!

KATE. Yee hah! (*They embrace.*)

THUNDER. So sorry about Loftus.

KATE. Yes, we found him in a cactus patch with a woman of easy virtue and a bottle of Jim Beam nearby.

THUNDER. (*Aghast.*) You mean?

KATE. Yes—cactus interruptus.

THUNDER. Well, it was the way Loftus would've wanted it. Did he have any final words? Any statement on the human condition?

KATE. Yes, he said "Roll your leg over, roll your leg over, oh roll your leg over, it's better that way."

THUNDER. Ah, Loftus, enigmatic to the end.

KATE. (*Brightening, somehow against all odds.*) So! What're you doing here in Muleshoe, you old horney toad!

EPHRAIM. Miss Katherine! Remember, we are trying to be a lady.

KATE. Watch it, Ephraim, I *am* a lady.

EPHRAIM. Of course you are, but it was part of your father's will that as the first lady of the territory you should beget a more lady-like demeanor.

KATE. Hey, look, I been back East and I can put on the fancy airs and manners of a lady anytime I've a mind to. I just don't happen to have a mind to.

EPHRAIM. Remember the will.

KATE. Right—the will.

EPHRAIM. And what was your father's dying wish?

KATE. To obey you in any and all things.

THUNDER. What hold has this man of God got over you niece?

EPHRAIM. She must follow the dictates of the Church of Christian Suffering and Denial. (*Aside.*) I should know. I wrote the will myself.

KATE. But enough of me! Dear uncle, what news of your son, my cousin Harry? I ain't laid eyeballs on him since I was knee-high to a corn muffin.

THUNDER. Harry! My son Harry! He's a dude. A dandy. He reads books. But West Point'll make a man of him.

CROW. Not necessarily, Colonel darlin'.

THUNDER. What do you mean?

CROW. Your son.

THUNDER. What about him?

CROW. Trying to keep it from you.

THUNDER. Keep what?

CROW. The truth.

THUNDER. Which is?

CROW. He's been kicked out of West Point.

THUNDER. (*Stricken.*) Booted from the Point? A father's hopes dashed.

KATE. That's tough luck about Harry and the Point. I always had a queer feeling in my gut that I'd end up marrying my first cousin. Call it woman's intuition.

THUNDER. (*Aside.*) Palpatating pulsating prairie dogs, she likes my son Harry.

KATE. (*Aside.*) I fear I am just wild about Harry. But growing up on a ranch I know more about the farm animals than I do about men. Understand, of course, I've got the basics down.

CROW. (*Aside.*) What is the Colonel up to? I fear, oh I fear!

THUNDER. (*Aside.*) My brother left her a wealthy woman. I'll arrange a marriage between her and my son!

EPHRAIM. (*Aside.*) He's plotting something, I know it! Because *I'm* plotting something.

THUNDER. (*Toasting.*) To the happy reunion of our two families.

ALL. To the families!

KATE. To Harry—

THUNDER. (*Aside.*) Gotta find him!

KATE. (*Aside.*) Wanna meet him!

EPHRAIM. (*Aside.*) Wanna save him!

CROW. (*Aside.*) Never met him!

THUNDER. To Harry!

ALL. To Harry! (*They all exit.*)

BLACKOUT

Scene 2

In front of a boarding house. Enter Harry Thunder, a dandyish youth. Muz, a ranch hand, stands holding Harry's luggage.

HARRY. Come along, Muz, and careful of my wardrobe. It's good to smell the sagebrush again. (*He sneezes.*) Blast this hay fever! Born in the West, raised in the East. How many military schools have I been kicked out of, Muz?

MUZ. Five. And now West Point. The Colonel's gonna whip me three ways to Sunday.

HARRY. Ah, Muz, I wasn't cut out to be a military man. All that shooting. Shocking. And the uniforms are so unimaginative. Muz, if only I'd been raised in the West. (*He sneezes.*) Been a man of the West. (*He sneezes.*) Then I should've been more like my friend Jack Rover. Jack Rover, whom I love better than a brother.

MUZ. You don't have a brother.

HARRY. Twit. Don't you think I know that.

MUZ. All I know is the Colonel's gonna blow his stack when he hears about the great shame you've brought upon the family name of Thunder.

HARRY. You mean getting kicked out of West Point.

MUZ. Worse! You've involved yourself in am immoral profession! Full of perverts and deviations. You've become an actor.

HARRY. True. I've become a thespian.

MUZ. That's what I mean. A profession of pederasts and thespians. It's disgusting.

HARRY. Muz.

MUZ. Besides, you're a man. You can't even be a thespian.

HARRY. Muz, I'm already a thespian.

MUZ. No wonder you got kicked out of West Point.

HARRY. Muz, a thespian is an actor.

MUZ. Still, play-acting under this assumed name of Dick Buckskin and not just play-acting, but Shakespearin'!

HARRY. I have definitely picked up the acting bug.

MUZ. You better hope that's all you've picked up. I've seen you with those actresses in the company.

HARRY. Well, good god, Muz, a fellow's got to sow some wild oats before settling down, before they clap you in irons.

MUZ. It's not the sowing I'd worry about if I were you, it's the clap!

HARRY. Those days are behind me now. I do not intend to rejoin the company in Deadwood. I intend to return home and face the music with my father. "Our revels now are ended."

MUZ. Aaarggh!

HARRY. What's the matter now?

MUZ. Quotatation.

11

HARRY. Quotatation?

MUZ. You've taken to quotatation like Mr. Rover. Every few seconds he's quotatating. Shakespeare this. Shakespeare that.

HARRY. True. It's his only fault. Rover's a simple son of the West come East to seek his fortune. He found Shakespeare and became drunk on the wine of his great word-music.

MUZ. Quotatation! I hates it!

HARRY. By the way, where is Rover?

MUZ. I think he's still in there diddlin' with the upstairs maid.

ROVER. (*Offstage.*) "I am dying, Egypt, dyin. . . . GGGGGG . . ." (*Jack Rover bounds out of the upstairs window of the boarding house, barechested, his shirt in his hand, with a beautiful girl, the Innkeeper's daughter. She holds a rose.*)

DAUGHTER. Quick! Before my father finds us. (*Rover holds her in his arms.*)

ROVER. "Goodnight, goodnight! Parting is such sweet sorrow that I shall say goodnight till it be morrow." (*Rover looks up, checking the sun.*) It be. (*Rover kisses the girl. She swoons. Rover bounds down. He pauses at the bottom of the stairs; blows her a kiss. She tosses him the rose. He joins Harry, D.*) Hi there, Dick. Morning, Muz. Sorry I'm late. I was just taking care of the upstairs maid.

HARRY. I'll bet you were.

ROVER. No, no. You don't understand. I got downstairs and I realized I'd put my shirt on over my suspenders. They were all tangled. Well naturally I had to change . . .

HARRY. Naturally.

MUZ. Naturally.

ROVER. So I went upstairs—

MUZ. He went upstairs.

ROVER. I took off my shirt.

HARRY. He took off his shirt.

ROVER. Well, what do you think—

HARRY/MUZ/ROVER. There's a girl in the room.

ROVER. How'd you guess.

HARRY. A shot in the dark.

ROVER. Well, one thing led to another, pretty soon she was helping me straighten my suspenders.

HARRY. She helped you straighten your suspenders? Did she? Sounds like a long story.

ROVER. Well, they were dangling.

HARRY. But did you get the situation well in hand?

ROVER. Well, working together—

MUZ. You got something straight between you.

ROVER. What?

HARRY. The suspenders.

ROVER. Right. In fact, maybe I better go back in there an give her a bigger tip.

HARRY. No, Jack, the road calls.

ROVER. You're right! We've got to get on the road again! Rejoin the company! What play are we doing in Deadwood tonight? I hope it's not *Lear*. I was devilish imperfect as Edgar the other night. (*He declaims.*) "The foul fiend haunts poor Tom in the voice of the nightingale."

MUZ. Quotatation!

ROVER. So! Which way to Deadwood, Dick?

HARRY. I'm not going to Deadwood, Jack.

ROVER. Not going to Deadwood, Dick?

HARRY. No. Not going to Deadwood, Jack.

ROVER. You're joking?

HARRY. No.

ROVER. I get it! Strike out on our own, eh? You're right! The devil with these provincial tours. Where shall we head, Dick? The big time? Tombstone, Waxahatchie, Hova Hova Nola?

HARRY. My dear fellow, on this road we must part.

ROVER. Part? But I'm going with you! Wherever you're headed I'm a-gonna follow.

HARRY. Jack, you and I have often met on a stage in assumed characters. If it's your wish we should ever meet again in our real ones of sincere friends, do not ask me of my motives or my destination. When I walk up this road, you must not follow.

ROVER. Joke, Dick?

HARRY. I wish it were, Jack. (*They embrace. Muz weeps.*)

ROVER. "Since my dear soul were mistress of her choice. And could of men distinguish, her election hath sealed thee for herself."

HARRY. ". . . And I will wear him in my heart's core, aye in my heart of heart, as I do thee."

ROVER. "Something too much of this."

13

MUZ. You said it! (*Harry exits.*)

ROVER. "Good night, sweet prince, and flights of angels sing thee to they rest!"

MUZ. Quotatation! I hates it! I hates it! (*Muz sighs. Rover sighs and exits in the opposite direction.*)

SCENE 3

The ranch houses of Gammon and Morales. Gammon and Ephraim enter from Gammon's.

EPHRAIM. So, Gammon, it's agreed — your daughter Jane is to come and work at the home of Katherine Thunder as her personal servant.

GAMMON. Agreed. Glad to get rid of her.

EPHRAIM. She will be well fed, well clothed — dresses, undergarments, garter belts.

GAMMON. I don't care about that. As long as I get her salary of $25 a week. She's a good worker, she's worth it. For another two bucks I'll throw in my son, Sim.

EPHRAIM. The boy is of no use to us. We only have enough underwear for the girl.

GAMMON. Well, drag me in the bushes and leave me for ripe. I think you got an eye for my daughter, Mr. Smooth.

EPHRAIM. Mr. Gammon, I am a man of God.

GAMMON. Well, then I won't insult you with a twenty dollar gold piece for taking the girl in.

EPHRAIM. Then insult me with *two* twenty dollar gold pieces. Have a pleasant day, Mr. Gammon.

GAMMON. It's too late for that. (*Sim enters, pushing a wheelbarrow.*) Sim! Put that wheelbarrow down. What do you know about machinery.

SIM. Well, I —

GAMMON. Where were you going?

SIM. Well, I —

GAMMON. Well, forget it. Call your sister.

SIM. (*Shouting.*) Hey sister! Hey sis!

GAMMON. Boy, if I put your brains in a bluebird, it'd fly backwards. (*Jane enters. A very spunky girl.*)

14

JANE. Yes, my dim-witted brother. You hollered.

GAMMON. Jane, you're to go to work for Miss Thunder up at the big house.

JANE. Do I have to join that weird religion—what's it called again?

EPHRAIM. The Church of Christian Suffering and Denial.

JANE. Sounds awful.

EPHRAIM. I'll initiate you into the Church—personally. Heh, heh, heh.

JANE. I hate it when he goes heh, heh, heh. (*Ephraim exits.*)

GAMMON. Quit your yammerin', girl, and listen to me, the both of you. (*Sweetly.*) Remember how I once told you the day must come when all the little chickies must leave the nest?

SIM. Yes, father.

JANE. Yes, father.

GAMMON. Well, today's chickie-day. We're gettin' rid of all the chickens.

SIM. (*Irate.*) But we can't do that! We can't get rid of the chickens! If we get rid of the chickens—where we gonna get the eggs! And I love eggs! Scrambled eggs, fried eggs, poached eggs! They're my favorite food! No, sir! I'm puttin' my foot down! The chickens stay!

JANE. Brother, the chickens aren't going anywhere.

SIM. (*Delighted.*) They're not!

JANE. We're the ones that are going.

GAMMON. That's right. I'm giving you the boot.

SIM. The boot? What boot?

GAMMON. Jane, pack your bags.

JANE. (*Nobly.*) Anything's better than living like this.

SIM. What boot? Am I just gonna get one?

GAMMON. Once I get rid of you two mewling brats I'll be able to marry Mr. Morales' sister! Women don't want to marry into a family with kids. Don't blame 'em. What's this? Someone out on the road. Sim, go see what they want.

SIM. Sim do this. Sim do that. And for what? One lousy boot. (*Sim exits. Gammon regards the Morales' adobe.*)

JANE. Amelia Morales! I knew it! Go on, admit it! You've lusted after her for years.

GAMMON. I have lusted after her for years.

JANE. What mischief are you plotting against the Morales's?

GAMMON. Mischief? Me?

JANE. I happen to know you've bought up all of Senor Morales' debtors notes in town.

GAMMON. You're a smart girl, Jane. Too smart. Well, since you know that, I'll tell you. I want Morales' sister and I mean to have her. If Morales doesn't consent, I'll have the Sheriff throw him in jail.

JANE. (*Crying.*) Oh, to have such a father. (*She exits. Sim enters. Senor Morales come out of his adobe.*)

SIM. Well, the feller says he's a Mister Kliegle and a Mister Leako. They run a pack of travellin' show folk.

GAMMON. Showfolk! Degenerates, drunkards and thieves. Can't abide 'em.

SIM. They want to rent the barn.

GAMMON. How much?

SIM. $25.00.

GAMMON. Well, don't just stand there cactus-brain. Go tell 'em it's a deal before they rent someplace else! Move! (*Sim exits. Morales comes up to Gammon.*)

MORALES. Buenos dios, Senor. Nice boy.

GAMMON. What brings you by, Morales.

MORALES. Well, Senor, I have a request.

GAMMON. I hope it's not about extending your loan?

MORALES. Si, Senor, it is.

GAMMON. That's too bad. But maybe we can work something out. Tell you what I'm going to do, Morales, what if I were to say you could wipe your debt clean in one fell swoop?

MORALES. How is that possible?

GAMMON. By telling me when I am to marry your sister.

MORALES. (*Stiffening.*) Why don't you ask Amelia yourself.

GAMMON. I have and she says she won't.

MORALES. Then it is certain she will not. She has a will of iron that woman.

GAMMON. What right has desert trash like you to talk so high and mighty to me?

MORALES. I may be poor, Senor, but my sister and I are not trashes.

GAMMON. I could make things very difficult for you, Morales. (*Rover enters.*)

ROVER. Howdy.

16

MORALES. Buenos dios.

ROVER. Hot day. Wonder if my horse and I could water down?

GAMMON. Horse?

ROVER. Tied to that cottonwood yonder.

GAMMON. That cottonwood's mine.

ROVER. Huh?

GAMMON. The land's mine. The water's mine. Even the gila monsters is mine! You're trespassin', hombre. (*Gammon enters house.*)

ROVER. "What a brazen face varlet art thou! . . . Come you rogue for though it be night, yet the moon shines, I'll make a sop o'the moonshine of you."

MORALES. You talk funny, Senor.

ROVER. Refusing water to a stranger in this country's criminal.

MORALES. Come Senor, you may drink from my well. It is not as cool and deep and sweet but it is as wet as water ever gets.

ROVER. "If there is a gentler soul in all of Christendom I have not met him yet."

MORALES. You're not from around here, are you? (*Rover and Morales go around behind the adobe. Gammon emerges from the house with Jane, her bag packed. He has her forcibly by the arm.*)

JANE. Owww!!!

GAMMON. Quit flappin' your trap! And not a word about this Morales business or I'll pull your ears off and use 'em for potholders. Ah! Here comes the Sheriff! And jumpin' jehosophat — Kate Thunder right behind him! (*The Sheriff enters.*)

SHERIFF. Mornin' Gammon.

GAMMON. That's enough out of you. Now as soon as Kate Thunder leaves we throw Morales in the clink before the Marshall gets back. (*We hear a thunder of hooves.*)

KATE. (*Offstage.*) YEEEE HAH!!!

EPHRAIM. (*Offstage scream.*) Yeeee HAHHHHH!!!!

KATE. Whoa! (*Kate strides in manfully. A shaken Ephraim follows her.*) Howdy! Are you Jane?

JANE. Yes ma'am.

KATE. I'm Kate Thunder.

JANE. Pleased to meet you. And this is my brother Sim.

KATE. (*To Jane.*) Is inbreedig a problem in your family?

SIM. Inbreeding? No ma'am. We do all our breeding out in the corral.

KATE. Are you the girl's father?

GAMMON. So her mother said!

KATE. Whew! Jane, how would you like to come work for me?

JANE. Oh, I'd love to! But I couldn't pay you very much in the beginning.

KATE. come along, Jane, Ephraim and I will discuss your duties.

EPHRAIM. Dresses, undergarments, garter belts. (*They enter the house.*)

GAMMON. Sure was good to meet ya! (*To Sheriff.*) Quick! Serve your warrant! Throw Morales in the clink! Ha-ha-ha-ha! (*Rover and Morales re-enter with buckets of water. Gammon continues laughing.*)

MORALES. Ah, he's in a good mood for once.

SHERIFF. Morales, you're under arrest.

MORALES. This is a day I have been dreading.

SHERIFF. Mr. Gammon here bought up all your debts. If you can't pay him fifty-five dollars it's off to the hoose-gow with you.

GAMMON. It's the law! It's the law! (*Kate, Jane, Ephraim re-enter, stand in the doorway, unnoticed by Rover.*)

ROVER. But it's an outrage! Surely in this land of abundance, wealth should flow like melting snow and trickle down to the valley below.

MORALES. I've heard of this trickle down theory. But you notice I'm still raising cactus. Only a miracle can save me now.

ROVER. A miracle — or me. (*Taking out his purse.*) Here Gammon! Here's fifty dollars — the last money I have in the world — now won't you forget the other five and let this old vaquero go?

GAMMON. No!

ROVER. "Villainy, villainy, villainy, I think upon't. I think I smel't. O villainy."

KATE. (*Aside.*) What beautiful sentiments he spoke just now. What is the meaning of this? I would ask what is the meaning of life — but we'd be here all day.

ROVER. Madame, this man won't even lift a finger to help his own neighbor and a kindlier soul I never met. My blood boileth over at the thought of it! My blood boileth over! My blood—(*He does a double-take to Kate. Their eyes lock.*)

KATE. Boileth over. (*Celestial music is heard as they stagger towards each other weak in the knees, loose in the limbs, their stomachs all aquiver.*)

ROVER. (*Aside.*) She's a goddess.

KATE. (*Aside.*) He's beautiful.

ROVER. (*Aside.*) Either I'm in love or I'm coming down with something real bad. (*To Kate.*) Hello.

KATE. Hello.

ROVER. Do you believe in love at first sight?

KATE. No. Do you?

ROVER. Of course not.

KATE. On the other hand, when you step barefoot into a cow patty, it may be warm and unexpected but you know for sure you've stepped in something. (*Rover tries to get it together.*)

ROVER. Ahhh ... yes. Well, you see, my old buddy here—what's your name again?

MORALES. Morales.

ROVER. Senor Morales got a little behind in his payments because of—because of—

MORALES. A bad cactus crop.

ROVER. Yes, you see, Mr. Morales—Senor Morales, that is—sells cactus, cacti actually ...

MORALES. Actually, I make tequilla.

ROVER. (*Aside.*) Quiet! She's obviously religious!

SHERIFF. (*To Morales.*) This man, Miss, has unpaid debts.

GAMMON. (*To Rover.*) And this man tried to prevent this officer of the law from doing his duty. (*Rover throws his arms around Morales.*)

MORALES. Begging your pardon, Miss, but I must interrupt. I am too proud to let my problems become a stranger's burden.

KATE. You mean you don't know this man?

ROVER. Ah shucks, I didn't do much.

MORALES. Didn't do much? He gave me fifty dollars! Gold!

ROVER. I could see in his eyes he was an honest man. (*To Kate.*) Sometimes by looking into a person's eyes you know all you'll ever need to know. (*Kate puts her hand to her neck and emits a tiny gasp.*) I only did what I felt was right.

KATE. Much obliged, stranger, but these humble tenants are my responsibility. Ephraim, write out a check to cover this man's debt.

EPHRAIM. Madame, I hardly think—

KATE. I know you don't. Write the check! (*Aside.*) Perhaps I shouldn't have told him that. For now he knows I'm rich.

ROVER. (*Aside.*) Perhaps I shouldn't have told her that for now she knows I'm poor. Oh what's the use. I'm a penniless player and she's a fine, wealthy lady with one of the best bodies I've ever seen. (*They look at each other. Sigh. Turn away. The piano player plays the main theme of Tchaikovsky's* "Romeo and Juliet."* (*Rover kneels, kisses her hand, rises.*) Adieu, adieu, remember me! (*Exits. Returns. Exits opposite direction.*) "Run, run Orlando, carve on every tree the fair, the chaste, the inexpressive she."

KATE. Who was that boy in buckskin?

SCENE 4

The bar.
Rover at the bar. Various card-players, dance hall girls, etc.

ROVER. (*Melancholia—to audience.*) "There is a tide in the affairs of men."—I shall not go to Deadwood. To have lost a friendship like Dick Buckskin. We were close. Very close. We never did anything disgusting but we were very close. But oh, that religious lady whom I saw today. If ever I gazed upon perfection it was in that face. A face that I shall never see again. My God, if only I could pay for these drinks. (*Enter Jane and Sim.*)

SIM. Oh sister, enter not into this den o' sin.

JANE. Sim, I'm here on a mission for Miss Katherine.

ROVER. Uh oh, here's two calves who've strayed from pasture.

JANE. Oh sir, there you are.

ROVER. What are you two doing in here?

JANE. My lady wishes to see you.

---

*See Special Note on copyright page.

ROVER. Well, I wish to see your lady.

JANE. (*Coyly.*) Ohhh ... perhaps you'd like to send her ladyship a kiss. You could give me the kiss, I could give it to my brother, Sim, and he could give it to my lady. (*Rover begins to flirt playfully with Jane.*)

ROVER. "No way but this killing myself to die upon a kiss!"

JANE. (*Swooning.*) Ohhhh!

SIM. (*Interposing.*) Hey, this is going far enough!

ROVER. Give your lady this—(*He kisses her chastely. She swoons.*)

JANE. Oh, my.

SIM. Why, you done kissed the legs right out from under her. (*Gammon enters as Jane exits.*)

JANE. Hello, father.

GAMMON. Hello, daughter. What the—(*But she is gone. Gammon accosts Sim.*) What the hell are you doin' lettin' her in a place like this? Not one day out of my house and she's taken to whorin'! And me not gettin' any percentage.

SIM. This here's my pa.

ROVER. "Take him for all in all; we shall not look upon his like again."

SIM. Well, let's hope not.

GAMMON. Shut up your mouth. (*To Rover.*) And as for you, I ain't forgettin' you crossed me. I got half a mind to whup knots on your head faster'n you can rub 'em. (*To Sim.*) Now where's that showman wants to hire my barn? I was told he was here.

SIM. I wouldn't know daddy, I—(*To Rover.*) Wait a minute now. You're one of the play-actors I seen over in Dry Gulch last week. You were in the play where the kids got to kick the mean old father out into the storm.

ROVER. *King Lear.*

SIM. Oh, that was a funny one!

ROVER. Funny?

SIM. I laughed till I cried.

ROVER. Well, not the usual response to *Lear.*

SIM. Do a little of it.

ROVER. "Blow winds and crack your cheeks!"

GAMMON. I'll crack both your cheeks. (*Gammon raises his whip to Rover; they wrestle. Sim steps in between them.*)

SIM. Stop! I can't let you beat my daddy.

GAMMON. I ain't forgettin' this! And I'm puttin' you on my list, bub! (*Gammon leaves.*)

ROVER. Do you love your daddy then, boy?

SIM. Love? Don't know. But I couldn't let you beat him.

ROVER. Why not?

SIM. Cause . . . he's my daddy.

ROVER. "Tho' love cool, friendship fall off. Brothers divide, subjects rebel. Oh! Never let the sacred bond be cracked twixt father and son." I never knew a father's protection. Never had a father to protect. "My father. Me thinks I see my father." (*He puts a handkerchief to his eyes.*)

SIM. Mister, are you play-acting again?

ROVER. Go on, son, you had better go find your daddy.

SIM. You're right. What's your name? In case I get to see you play act again.

ROVER. (*Theatrically.*) My name? Why—"I am the Bold Thunder."

SIM. Oh mister, I love it when you versify.

ROVER. "Thunder, lightning. You cataracts and huricanos!" (*Sim leaves laughing and crying.*) Barkeep, give me a shot. "I am the Bold Thunder." (*There is a flash from offstage.*)

KLIEGLE. (*Offstage.*) Illuminating, Mr. Leako.

LEAKO. (*Offstage.*) Incandescent, Mr. Kliegle.

ROVER. Say, who all's in the back room, barkeep?

BARTENDER. A Mister Kleigle and a Mister Leako.

ROVER. Kliegle and Leako! I know the scaliwags. A couple of lightweight theatrical impresarios, determined to invent a lighting box to replace gaslight. Can you imagine? Ha-ha-ha. (*An explosion offstage. Enter Kliegle and Leako in aprons holding smoking, exploded lighting instruments.*)

KLIEGLE. Less than illuminating, Mr. Leako.

LEAKO. Less than incandescent, Mr. Kliegle.

KLIEGLE. Back to the drawing board, Mr. Leako?

LEAKO. Back to the drawing board, Mr. Kliegle!

ROVER. But perhaps they need a leading man. "Oh I am fortune's fool." (*He follows them to the back room. Crow enters.*)

CROW. When does the noon stage leave?

BARTENDER. Four o'clock.

CROW. Good. I've got time for a drink, and I'd like to book passage for myself and Colonel Thunder.

BARTENDER. Thunder? Why Mister Thunder's in the back room now with a couple of show folk.

CROW. Mister Thunder? Impossible. I just left Mister Thunder—wait—show folk? Could it be the young Mister Harry whom I—through a string of amazing coincidences—have never seen? (*From the back room enter Rover, Kliegle, Leako, Gammon, and Sim.*)

KLIEGLE. Have we seen the light, Mr. Leako?

LEAKO. Dawn is breaking, Mr. Kliegle.

KLIEGLE. We'll perform the play in your barn then, Mr. Gammon.

GAMMON. Yeah, agreed. Fifty dollars! And nobody had oughta try to cheat me out of my fee! C'mom, Sim. (*They exit.*)

KLIEGLE. How de*light*ful, Mr. Leako.

LEAKO. Luminous idea, Mr. Kliegle.

KLIEGLE. We've obtained the services of Mr. Rover here.

LEAKO. But come, Mr. Kliegle, we must prepare for the performance.

KLIEGLE. Shine *on*, Mr. Leako.

LEAKO. De*light*ed, Mr. Kliegle.

CROW. Is that him?

BARTENDER. That's Mr. Thunder, yes.

CROW. Harry!

ROVER. What?

CROW. Harry! Harry!

ROVER. Where? Where?

CROW. Ah, you're the spitting image of your father. You look just like the Colonel.

ROVER. The Colonel?

CROW. Don't pretend you don't know who the Colonel is.

ROVER. Tarnation and thunder!

CROW. That's right, Thunder. By the way, we know about your flunking out of West Point.

ROVER. We do?

CROW. And then there's you rich cousin, Kate, your father wants you to marry.

ROVER. There is?

CROW. Course you haven't seen each other for years.

ROVER. We haven't?

CROW. Oh no. But she's dying to see you.

23

ROVER. She is?

CROW. Come, let's be about it.

ROVER. Look. I'm not who you think I am. I'm an actor.

CROW. Well . . . aren't we all in the larger sense. You can give a private performance for the fine lady.

ROVER. What am I? A chimp on a chain to perform for the rich? Am I a man or a monkey?

BARTENDER. How're you gonna pay for this bar bill?

ROVER. Pass the bananas.

CROW. That's the spirit.

ROVER. Amazing the vicissitudes of fortune. Is she pretty?

CROW. She could raise a corpse. I should know.

ROVER. Will this Colonel be there?

CROW. Not if we hurry.

ROVER. "Once more unto the breech!" "Frailty thy name is woman." "The quality of mercy is not strained!" "My horse, my horse, My kingdom for a horse!" Picture if you will a melancholy Dane — "To be, or not to be — that is the question." (*Rover exits.*)

CROW. The boy's a raving lunatic. He's the Colonel's son all right. (*Crow exits.*)

SCENE 5

Kate Thunder's drawing room. A canvas curtain rolls down disguising the bar. Kate and Ephraim Smooth going over the account books, checking off names.

EPHRAIM. But madame, we must foreclose.

KATE. But why?

EPHRAIM. Because all of your tenants owe you money.

KATE. But shouldn't we be helping the poor like that incredibly handsome stranger? Aren't we supposed to me meek and humble and all?

EPHRAIM. Madame, we must collect in the name of the Church of Christian Suffering and Denial. The roads abound with robbers and thieves. Why, the Church has even offered a reward for one of these bandits. We must protect the women, the young women, and the very young women. Hallelujah! (*Jane enters.*)

KATE. Well, you took your own sweet time about getting here. Did you find him?

JANE. He's so handsome, ma'am.

KATE. We know that.

JANE. So tall, ma'am.

KATE. We know that, too. Did you tell him to come here?

KATE. He kissed me, ma'am.

EPHRAIM. (*Aside.*) The saucy hussy seems to have fallen for the lout. (*They exit.*)

KATE. Well, this is a fine how-do-y'do. The poor girl's lost her heart. (*Rapturously.*) But who could blame her? True, he was shabbily dressed; true, he needed better boots. But wasn't he generous? Wasn't he kind? Wasn't he built like a Greek God? Oh black-eyed peas and cornbread! I'd better get hold of myself. He could be anyone. He could be here to steal my inheritance. As if I wouldn't give him that and my heart as well. (*Crow enters.*)

CROW. Madame, I have returned.

KATE. I can see that, and without knocking.

CROW. Sorry ma'am! I have your cousin Harry here.

KATE. My cousin Harry! Here in Muleshoe.

CROW. Here and in the flesh. May I present your cousin Harry . . . Cousin Harry! (*Rover bounds into the room in traditional Hamlet garb: black tights, black doublet, gold chain around his neck, carrying a skull.*)

ROVER. "Tis I, Hamlet the Dane."

KATE. Oh, my God.

ROVER. Oh, my God.

KATE. (*Aside.*) The handsome stranger!

ROVER. (*Aside.*) The lovely lady!

KATE. My cousin Harry?

ROVER. Where? Where?

CROW. (*Aside to Rover.*) It's your cousin Katherine, boy. Your father has his heart set on this marriage. Court her, you mad devil you! (*Crow exits.*)

ROVER. (*Aside.*) He thinks I'm her cousin. Oh, and she's so refined. I'd better be on my best behavior. (*He strikes a pose of savior faire.*)

KATE. (*Aside.*) He quotes Shakespeare; he must be very high-toned. I'd better put on my best Bryn Mawr accent. I wonder where I left it?

25

ROVER. Well, it's . . . it's . . . it's been a long time.

KATE. Yes, it has. Veddy long. Veddy, veddy long.

ROVER. Yes, uh, how long *has* it been?

KATE. We haven't seen each other since we were eight years old. So . . . what have you been doing with yourself?

ROVER. Oh, this and that.

ROVER and KATE. (*Aside.*) How long can I keep this up?

ROVER. Cousin Katherine.

KATE. I do wish you'd call be Kate. (*She extends her hand; he his. Unfortunately, his hand still has the skull in it.*)

ROVER. Oh, my.

KATE. Oh, dear.

ROVER. So sorry.

KATE. A skull, isn't it?

ROVER. Yes. Just a skull.

KATE. No one in the family, I hope.

ROVER. Ha-ha-ha. No, no . . . "Alas, poor Yorick."

KATE. Why're you carrying it, if I may ask?

ROVER. (*Weakly.*) Don't you ever get the urge to dress up like Hamlet and carry around a skull?

KATE. No.

ROVER. She probably thinks I'm mad.

KATE. I should probably think you mad if eccentricity didn't run in our family.

ROVER. Runs in the family?

KATE. Practically gallops. When we met earlier why didn't you tell me you were the son of my uncle Croftus Thunder?

ROVER. Good question. (*Aside.*) Because I didn't know myself—(*To Kate.*) Because I didn't recognize *you.*

KATE. (*Reaching for her purse.*) I must repay you for the Morales' debt.

ROVER. No, no. Really.

KATE. No, no. I insist.

ROVER. I can't.

KATE. You must.

ROVER. I shan't.

KATE. You shall.

ROVER. My pride.

KATE. Mine too.

ROVER. Can't accept.

KATE. Must accept.

ROVER. I shall not be indebted to one I — dare I say it? — love.

KATE. Dare.

ROVER. Love. "Perdition catch my soul, but I do love thee!"

KATE. Cousin. This is so sudden.

ROVER.

"O, she doth teach the torches to burn bright!
It seems she hangs upon the check of night
Like a rich jewel in an Ethiop's ear,
Beauty too rich for use, for earth too dear!"

KATE. (*Blushing modestly.*) Well, I am the prettiest girl in Muleshoe.

ROVER. Muleshoe! Texas! The world! (*He kneels.*)

"If I profane with my unworthiest hand
This holy shrine, the gentle fine is this —
My lips two blushing Pilgrims, ready stand
To smooth that rough touch with a tender kiss."

(*He is about to kiss her hand. He rises violently.*) But I do profane! I do! "I am not what I am!"

KATE. What am you? I mean, what are you?

ROVER. A fraud. These clothes, my manners, . . .

KATE. (*Dreamily.*) Your shoulders, your eyes . . .

ROVER. Everything I've ever learned! Originate from one source — I owe it all to Shakespeare.

KATE. Huh?

ROVER. When you know the truth — my name is —

KATE. Harry Thunder.

ROVER. (*Aside.*) I must not lie to her! I must tell the truth. I must tell her my name is Rover. (*To Kate.*) No, my name is Harry Thunder. (*Aside.*) What can I do? When she knows who I am I lose her. If only there were some way out of this! If only there would come a-knocking at the door. (*There comes a-knocking at the door.*) Enter! (*Enter Kliegle, Leako and Gammon.*)

KLIEGLE. Ah, there you are Mr. Rover! In the limelight, Mr. Leako.

LEAKO. In the spotlight, Mr. Kliegle.

ROVER. (*Aside.*) Out of the frying pan into the fire — (*To all.*) What is the meaning of this?

KLIEGLE. Why Mr. Rover, we're here with the contracts.

LEAKO. For the performance of the play.

GAMMON. To be held in my barn.

KATE. Who are these people, Harry?

ROVER. I've never seen them before in my life.

KLIEGLE and LEAKO. We're Kliegle and Leako Traveling Players.

KLIEGLE. You're to perform for us later this week, Mr. Rover.

ROVER. Rover? Rover? I am the Bold Thunder! Harry Thunder to be precise! Son of — son of —

KATE. Colonel Croftus Thunder!

ROVER. Thank you.

LEAKO. We'll be sued!

KLIEGLE. We'll go broke!

KLIEGLE and LEAKO. (*To Gammon.*) You won't get paid!

KLIEGLE. Please, sir, won't you reconsider?

ROVER. Never! Never! Never! (*Aside.*) Kate probably hates actors.

KATE. Oh, why don't you do it, cousin? I just love the theatre.

ROVER. In that case I accept. But I'm not Jack Rover. Do you understand?

KLIEGLE. Anything you say, sir.

LEAKO. Anything you say.

ROVER. And I refuse to perform in this man's barn.

GAMMON. What?

KLIEGLE and LEAKO. In that case, where will we perform the play?

KLIEGLE. Half-light befalls us, Mr. Leako.

LEAKO. Twilight, Mr. Kliegle.

KATE. You can perform the play in the saloon in town.

ROVER. The saloon?

KATE. I own it.

ROVER. Well, in that case . . .

KLIEGLE. Beaming, Mr. Leako.

LEAKO. Blazing, Mr. Kliegle.

KLIEGLE and LEAKO. We'll perform the play in your saloon in town.

GAMMON. Not in my barn?

LEAKO. How shining, Mr. Kliegle.

KLIEGLE. Heliotropic, Mr. Leako. (*They exit.*)

GAMMON. Mister, I'm about to kill you and tell God you

died! You done ripped your drawers with me, bub! I'm about to tear your arms out by the roots and beat you to death with 'em! I'm about to — I'm about to — (*Rover advances rather threateningly. Gammon backs down.*) I'm about to leave. I'm goin', but you ain't seen the last of Ike Gammon. (*Piano player plays villain music.*) Aw, don't bother. They get the point. (*He exits.*)
ROVER. Come, Kate. (*They exit.*)

SCENE 6

The Bar.
Harry and Muz at the bar. Harry signing the register.

MUZ. You signed your name "Dick Buckskin." I thought he was gone forever.
HARRY. So did I, Muz. But I want to lay low until you've talked to my father. See if he's in a scratchy mood. Well, this is a lively enough establishment. Look here, Muz, I'm going to go upstairs and dress for dinner. Fascinating establishment. You find out where my father's staying.
MUZ. Right, sir. (*Harry heads up the stairs. Thunder enters.*)
THUNDER. Crow! Tend to the mounts! I dally for only a spot of liquid refreshment. Then back to tracking those deserters.
MUZ. Sufferin' sidewinders, it's the Colonel! (*Muz tries to sneak past the Colonel but is apprehended.*)
THUNDER. Say, don't I know you?
MUZ. Oh no, sir. I've got one of those unfortunate faces you think you remember but you've never seen.
THUNDER. You've got a face like the south end of a north bound dog. I'd remember a face like that.
MUZ. No matter who you're thinking of — it wasn't me.
THUNDER. I'm thinkin' of a no good ranchhand of mine who had a face that was severly beaten with the ugly stick. I entrusted him with my son's conduct. If I find out my boy's been misbehavin' I'll take that worthless Muz and pull the varmit apart like a wishbone.
MUZ. (*Aside.*) I'd best warn Harry he's about to walk into an ambush. As for me, I'm gonna disappear from this play for the

29

better part of an hour. It was a good role while it lasted. (*Muz exits upstairs to Harry's room. Crow enters.*)

CROW. Colonel darlin'.

THUNDER. What the hell do you mean sneaking up on me like that?

CROW. I bring news of your son, sir!

THUNDER. My son!

CROW. He's here in Muleshoe.

THUNDER. Where?

CROW. He's even now at this moment walking and wooing in a garden with your niece Katherine.

THUNDER. Why, I'll kill him! I'll strangle him. I'll — my niece Katherine? The one that's so rich and I want him to marry?

CROW. The same. He's quite the ladies man.

THUNDER. Ready our mounts! There's not a moment to lose. (*Crow exits.*) I must eye this situation like a fox in a hen house to make certain my son handles this affair seriously — and that he's not just sowing wild oats. (*Enter Harry from above, disguised as a old man with plenty of whiskers.*)

HARRY. I hope this disguise fools my father till I can distinguish his mood — which is nearly always foul. (*He goes to the bar.*) Howdy, stranger!

THUNDER. Hello there. (*He does a take.*) Saints preserve us! I thought for a second I was being accosted by a walrus. You must be thirsty under all that fur, granddad. Can I buy you a drink?

HARRY. Thank you. So, what brings you to town, sonny?

THUNDER. Dastardly deserters, sir. From the glorious Seventh Cavalry! (*The piano player plays* "Gary Owens." *Thunder gives him a hard look. He plays a few bars of* "Misty.")* I'm determined to track 'em down.

HARRY. Highly commendable.

THUNDER. But my heart is weighted down with heavier issues. I have a son who's shortly to be married.

HARRY. Congratulations! (*Suddenly dawning.*) What the hell am I saying! I don't want to be married! You know, sir, a young man must sow his wild oats.

THUNDER. My son has sowed all the oats he's going to.

*See Special Note on copyright page.

HARRY. I haven't even begun to sow my oats. I mean, suppose your son doesn't want to marry the girl. Suppose she's ugly?

THUNDER. He'd marry the girl if she was ugly enough to make a freight train take a dirt road. Besides, nothing makes ugly pretty faster'n rich.

HARRY. I tell ya he won't marry her!

THUNDER. He'll do what he's told! He'll marry the girl if she looks like a pig! (*Harry snatches off his beard.*)

HARRY. Father, I refuse to marry this pig-woman!

THUNDER. Cowering Caterwauling Commanches! My progeny! What the hell are you doing here?

HARRY. Father, I know you're angry with me for being kicked out of West Point.

THUNDER. I don't give a damn about that.

HARRY. (*Aside.*) This gets stranger and stranger.

THUNDER. I hear you've got an eye for the lady?

HARRY. (*Aside.*) How did he hear about the actresses in the company? (*To Thunder.*) Well, sir, I confess there were a couple I was quite fond of.

THUNDER. A couple?

HARRY. Well, three or four.

THUNDER. Three or four? Good Lord, boy! You don't dally with the entire herd when the prize heifer is willing.

HARRY. What're you talking about?

THUNDER. Were you or were you not just this hour wooing Kate Thunder?

HARRY. Isn't she my cousin or something?

THUNDER. Consarn it! Of course she's your cousin.

HARRY. I haven't seen her since I was eight.

THUNDER. Either you or Crow is lyin'. (*Crow enters, whistling.*) Of course! Crow made all this up.

CROW. A quick drink, Colonel, and I'll take you to your son. (*To Harry.*) Top o'the morning to you, sir.

THUNDER. (*Sweetly.*) Crow.

CROW. Yes, Colonel darlin'.

THUNDER. Did you bring my son to my niece's?

CROW. That I did. That I did. And it was love at first sight.

THUNDER. (*To Harry.*) What do you have to say to that?

HARRY. False. He didn't bring your son anywhere.

31

CROW. And how would you know?

HARRY. And who should know better!

THUNDER. Something's amiss here. Perhaps you've met Kate Thunder and decided you weren't taken with her. It's *you* who rejects the marriage.

HARRY. What marriage?

THUNDER. That's the purpose of these tomfool whiskers! You hoped to break off a marriage that I've set my heart on!

HARRY. Sir—I'm confused.

THUNDER. Damn your confusion! Ingrate! Come, we're off to your cousin Kate's, where you're going to marry her and live happily ever after . . . or else!

CROW. What about the deserters?

THUNDER. Deserters? Plenty of time for them! Plenty of time! Why, when I set my mind on finding those deserters I'll find them like that! Like that, do you hear! Recognize 'em in a minute. (*Three evil-looking men, Wilson, Liberty and Angel Eyes, enter all dressed in Cavalry uniforms. The Colonel bumps into them.*)

LIBERTY. Hey, watch where you're going.

THUNDER. Beg pardon, didn't see you there. (*To Crow and Harry.*) CHARGE!!!!! (*The piano player strikes up "Gary Owens," and then shifts into the outlaw theme. The three outlaws clear the bar of everyone, then face the audience, guns drawn.*)

WILSON. Shall we shoot 'em now?

LIBERTY. Naw.

ANGEL EYES. Why not?

LIBERTY. Intermission. (*With that they shoot out the footlights, chandelier, and stage lights.*)

BLACKOUT

ACT TWO

Scene 1

The bar.
The piano player tinkling away softly. In walk the desperadoes.
They strut into the bar. From the other wings strut Gammon,
Sim and the Sheriff. The groups eye each other distrustfully.
Then they all come together barber-shop quartet style and sweetly
sing "Red River Valley."*

ALL.
"From this valley they say you are leaving
We will miss your bright eyes and sweet smile
For they say you are taking the sunshine
That has brightened our pathway a while"
LIBERTY. Everybody now!
ALL.
"So come sit by my side if you love me
Do not hasten to bid me adieu
But remember the Red River Valley
And the cowboy who loved you so true."
(*The song ended, the deserters and others face off once more. Wilson,*
Liberty and Angel Eyes take a table. All stare at them.)
GAMMON. (*Aside.*) Surely these are the army deserters I hear
tell Colonel Thunder has been following! (*Wilson rises and growls*
at him.)
ANGEL EYES. (*Grinning.*) Gettin' kind of edgy, ain't ya,
Wilson?
WILSON. I don't like it when they stare.
LIBERTY. Sure he's edgy. Who wouldn't be? We haven't killed
anybody since yesterday.
ANGEL EYES. That ain't what's eatin' at him, Liberty.
LIBERTY. Spit it out, Wilson.
WILSON. You said I could wear the black hat today.
LIBERTY. Did I?
WILSON. You promised.
LIBERTY. Why don't you try and take it, Wilson. (*They both*

*See Special Note on copyright page.

stand stealthily, their hand hovering over their guns.) Make your play, Wilson.

WILSON. You first, Liberty. (*Angel Eyes chuckles.*)

LIBERTY. What's so funny, Angel Eyes?

ANGEL EYES. I'm just thinking, I get to kill the winner. (*Gammon intercedes.*)

GAMMON. Gentlemen, gentlemen, there's no cause to shoot each other.

LIBERTY. Who needs a cause?

GAMMON. I know who you fellers are. You're the deserters.

WILSON. *Now we got a cause.*

GAMMON. No, no, wait. I'm in the position to do a little horse tradin'.

LIBERTY. What'd'ya mean, hombre?

GAMMON. There's someone doggin' your trail.

ANGEL EYES. Doggin my trail. If there's one thing I hate it's someone doggin' my trail.

GAMMON. And I can take you to him.

ANGEL EYES. There's nothing I hate worse than a man doggin' my trail.

LIBERTY. What do we have to do?

GAMMON. A favor. There's a certain lady here in town; a certain Miss Thunder, who if she were, well, indisposed— (*He begins to lead Liberty away from the group towards the back room. The others follow.*)

ANGEL EYES. I just *hate* a man doggin' my trail. (*They exit.*)

Scene 2

Kate's dressing room. Kate pacing before a dressing screen. She's dressed in the somber clothing of the Church of Christian Suffering and Denial.

KATE. Damn! If this ain't the fly in the buttermilk. I love my cousin Harry but I've lied to him. Oh, he thinks I'm some sort of high-fallutin' Bryn Mawr graduate. Well, I am and I ain't. I went back yonder to school, got inoculated with East Coast culture—it just didn't take, that's all . . . I gotta start actin' like myself again. And if he can't take me like I am he can just forget it! What if he forgets it? I'll lose my wild roving boy. (*Going into East Coast Kate accent.*) On the other hand, I can't go around talking like this the rest of my life. (*Western Kate.*) Oh to hell with it! Harry'll be here in three shakes of a lamb's tail to rehearse the play. I've gotta 'fess up and just be myself. (*Rover enters.*)

ROVER. Hello, Kate. How are you?

KATE. (*East Coast Kate.*) Veddy, veddy fine, thank you. (*Aside.*) Dang!!

ROVER. I say, it's awfully nice of you to fill in like this since one of our actresses took ill.

KATE. It's a pleasure, I'm sure.

ROVER. Although truthfully I'm a little nervous about acting with you.

KATE. Really? Why?

ROVER. In play-acting we often expose our true selves more than we know.

KATE. Sounds frightfully revelatory.

ROVER. It is.

KATE. I gotta do it. This is my chance to show my true colors.

ROVER. Are we ready to begin?

KATE. We're veddy, veddy ready. (*Aside.*) Dang, dang!! (*To Rover.*) But first, I must change clothes. (*She goes behind the screen.*)

ROVER. Change clothes?

KATE. (*Western Kate.*) Yeah, I'm sweatin' like a whore in church.

ROVER. Well, in that case I—what?

KATE. (*East Coast Kate.*) Nothing, nothing. Continue.

ROVER. I've got the perfect role for you—Rosalind in *As You Like It*. She's chaste, she's pure, she's virtuous.

KATE. (*Western Kate.*) Sounds like a tight-ass to me.

ROVER. Well, she's sort of a—what?

KATE. (*East Coast Kate.*) Continue, continue.

ROVER. Well, it's a hard role.

KATE. Harder than a preacher's pecker at a two-bride wedding? Ha-ha-ha. (*Realizing her error.*) I couldn't be more apologetic.

ROVER. Anyway—here's your script. (*She comes out from behind the screen in a Merry Widow's corset.*)

KATE. Thanks.

ROVER. On second thought — take a look at Kate in *Taming of the Shrew*.

KATE. Good, that fits my pistol a little bit better. (*Slaps where her pistol should be, realizes her state of undress and scampers back behind the screen.*)

ROVER. Fascinating woman! I'll come in over here.

KATE. Very well.

ROVER. On second thought, I'll come in over here.

KATE. All rightie.

ROVER. (*Seeing Kate.*) If God had made a better body he would have kept it for himself. I'll come in over here. (*Rehearsing.*) "Good morrow, Kate." "Good morrow, Kate." "Good . . . morrow Kate!" (*Kate bounds from behind the screen, book in hand, dressed in a sexy buckskin outfit.*)

KATE. "They call me Katherine that do talk of me."

ROVER. "You lie in faith, for you are called plain Kate, and bonny Kate, and sometimes Kate the curst. But Kate, the prettiest Kate in Christendom."

KATE. Have your eyes alway been that big?

ROVER. "Kate of Kate Hall."

KATE. And your lips that full?

ROVER. "My super dainty Kate . . ."

KATE. And your nose that bent?

ROVER. I got it in a fight, okay?

KATE. Okay.

ROVER. Moving right along . . .

KATE. "Moved! In good time let him that moved you hither . . ." Do you think Kate hates Petruchio? "The lady doth protest too much, methinks."

ROVER. My god, Kate! You really *do* know your Shakespeare! "Come and sit on me!" (*He sits on the stool. She sits on his lap.*) Ahhhhh . . .

KATE. Am I too heavy?

ROVER. Mmnn. No. Just right.

KATE. Shall I move?

ROVER. Don't you dare!

KATE. "Asses are made to bear and so are you."

ROVER. "Women are made to bear, and so are you."

KATE. Would you like a large family?

ROVER. Well . . . Uh . . . I . . . I think we should proceed with the scene. (*They rise.*) "Come, come, you wasp; i'faith you are too angry."

KATE. "If I be waspish, best beware my sting."

ROVER. "My remedy is then, to pluck it out."

KATE. "Ay, if the fool could find where it lies."

ROVER. "Who knows not where a wasp doth wear his sting? In his tail."

KATE. "In his tongue."

ROVER. "Whose tongue?"

KATE. "Yours, if you talk of tails; and so farewell."

ROVER. "What, with my tongue in your tail? Nay, good Kate: I am a gentleman." (*She strikes him. He kisses her.*) I swear I'll cuff you if you strike again.

KATE. Does she strike again?

ROVER. Yes. (*She strikes at him gently. He grabs her. They kiss more passionately. They kiss again, more passionately.*)

KATE. "Where did you study all this goodly . . . speech?"

ROVER. "It is extempore, from my mother wit."

KATE. "A witty mother! Witless else her son."

ROVER. "Am I not wise?"

KATE. "Yes, keep you warm."

ROVER. "Marry so I mean Katherine, in thy bed — for I am he am born to tame you, Kate . . . I must and will have Katherine to my wife." (*She kisses him.*) Why Kate, you've got passion! You've got spirit! You've got wazza-wazza-zoom-zoom-zoom!

KATE. And why shouldn't I have! Do you think men are the only ones allowed to sow their "wild oats"? (*She kisses him again.*) What do you have to say to *that?*

ROVER. "Oh brave new world! That has such people in't!" (*Enter Ephraim Smooth.*)

EPHRAIM. Miss Katherine? Miss Katherine? Oh, Miss Katherine!!! This house has become the Palace of Beelzebub! Actors everywhere. In the living room. In the study. In the kitchen. Always in the kitchen. And no one eats like an actor. (*Aside.*) Even Jane has taken a part. Oh brethren, I say to you the theatre is the breeding ground for whoremasters, pimps, trollopes, agents, producers, and sluts.

ROVER. That's ridiculous. Actors are not all whoremasters, trollopes and sluts. (*Enter Jane, dressed like a slut, script in hand.*)

JANE. "I am a slut! And I thank the Gods I am foul!"

ROVER. Of course, some of us are."

EPHRAIM. I am too late! Her conversion to sluttishness is complete.

ROVER. No. It's just a line from *As You Like It.* Uh, Jane, I think you should take a closer look at your text.

JANE. Oh, excuse me. Ahem. "I am *not* a slut, though I thank God I am foul."

ROVER. "Well, praised be the Gods for thy foulness! Sluttishness may come hereafter."

JANE. Good! Then I'll be a *real* actress.

EPHRAIM. Come, Jane. We must return to your instructions in the Church of Christian Suffering and Denial.

JANE. But I wish to deny nothing.

EPHRAIM. That's why you need more instruction. (*They exit.*)

ROVER. Ah. Now we are alone.

KATE. What shall we do?

ROVER. . . . You know.

KATE. No. I don't know.

ROVER. (*Crestfallen.*) I was hoping you did. I was hoping you would feel as I do. I was hoping two hearts would beat as one.

KATE. "I'll see thee hanged on Sunday first."

ROVER. Huh?

KATE. End of the Shrew scene.

ROVER. Right! "We will have rings and things and fine array, and kiss me Kate, we will be married a Sunday." (*They kiss.*)

KATE. Oh Harry! Harry Thunder. Mrs. Harry Thunder. (*As she exits.*) Little Harry Thunder. Little Harriet Thunder. Puppy Thunder.

ROVER. Zounds, I am lost. She thinks I'm Harry. Oh, connuptual connundrum. If only I had someone here to talk to — someone to confide in. Someone, someone . . . (*Enter Harry hurriedly.*)

HARRY. Thank God I've escaped my father's clutches for a moment.

ROVER. Someone like Dick Buckskin — good lord, Dick Buckskin!

HARRY. Jack Rover!

ROVER. How'd you know I was here? Oh, I get it! You saw the playbills. Name above the title . . . not bad, eh?

HARRY. (*Aside.*) He doesn't know who I am yet! I'll carry it through. (*To Rover.*) So! What play are you doing, Jack?

ROVER. Don't call me Jack. I am Jack Rover no more. I am now Cadet Harry Thunder of West Point.

HARRY. (*Aside.*) Good Lord, he's impersonating me!

ROVER. Oh Dick, I tell you I don't feel anything like myself.

HARRY. I shouldn't wonder. Have you been drinking?

ROVER. No, Dick, you see I met this ancient Indian with an Irish accent in an Army jacket.

HARRY. Were you taking drugs?

ROVER. Then he brought me to this house where I've fallen in love with the world's most beautiful woman.

HARRY. Do you have any more of these drugs?

ROVER. No, but the hitch is I'm supposed to be some idiot named Harry Thunder.

HARRY. (*Aside.*) He's talking about me! (*To Rover.*) An idiot, is he?

ROVER. Sure, all those rich high-falutin' fellows care about is their clothes. By the way, nice set of duds, Dick, makes you look a little like a yellow-bellied sap sucker.

HARRY. This suit happens to be the very height of fashion.

ROVER. Say, I've got a part for you tonight in *Taming of the Shrew*.

HARRY. Petruchio?

ROVER. No, that needs a really good actor! And besides, the woman playing Kate is the beautiful lady of the house.

HARRY. (*Aside.*) My cousin! And what does he mean, not a good actor? Does he love her? (*To Rover.*) Do you love her, Jack?

ROVER. To distraction, Dick. But she is the one I shall not have.

HARRY. (*Aside.*) That doesn't sound like Jack. (*To Rover.*) That doesn't sound like you, Jack.

ROVER. It's *not* like me, Dick. No, I've just decided! I'll perform the play as agreed, and then I'll bid her adieu and depart from the Forest of Arden forever.

HARRY. Damned decent of you, Jack.

ROVER. I know it is, Dick.

HARRY. (*Aside.*) Poor Jack, he's every inch a gentleman indeed. But wait—perhaps there's a way—yes—yes—(*To Rover.*)

Jack, I have a confession to make. I didn't come here to see the play.

ROVER. You didn't? I can get you comps.

HARRY. No! I came here for the very same purpose you did. To pass myself off as this very same Harry Thunder!

ROVER. No! What a coincidence!

THUNDER. (*Offstage.*) Harry! Harry, my boy!

ROVER. Who's that?

HARRY. My father—I mean—that is—the actor I've hired to play my father.

ROVER. You've hired an actor to play Colonel Thunder?

HARRY. Exactly! Kate hasn't seen her uncle in years. It was his idea to marry me off and split the inheritance. (*Aside.*) I'll bet *you* folks couldn't think this fast in a pinch!

THUNDER. (*Offstage.*) Harry! Where's my boy Harry?

ROVER. Why, this old actor must be a regular Falstaff—"A corrupter of youth." I love the lady and shall not see her harmed. This old actor of yours has roused my wrath. And you know what my wrath is like when it's roused.

HARRY. It's one of the last things we wish to see, Jack.

ROVER. I'm mad! Good and mad!

HARRY. Restrain your wrath a moment longer to take revenge and make it stronger. You be me and I'll be thee. We'll dupe him then with such confusion twill make him mad with our delusion.

ROVER. Come again?

HARRY. Just keep pretending you're Harry Thunder and I'll pretend not to know him. It'll drive him bonkers.

ROVER. (*Affecting a foppish manner.*) I wil lisp and drawl and affect the very image of gentility.

HARRY. Okay, but don't overdo it.

THUNDER. (*Offstage.*) Harry my boy!

HARRY. Quick! Behind the screen! I'll signal three stamps when you are to enter. (*Rover hides behind the screen.*) Rover doesn't have the slightest inkling he's imitating me. And doing a very poor job of it. But this affords an excellent opportunity of making my poor friend's fortune. If possible he shall have this lady. Ah, here she comes now. (*Enter Kate.*) Madame, a word with you.

KATE. Who are you, what are you doing here, and my God, what are you wearing?

40

HARRY. I'm a friend, I'm here to help you, and this suit happens to be the very height of fashion.

KATE. You look like a banana.

HARRY. We musn't talk. Time is of the essence.

KATE. Oh, they all say that.

HARRY. Do you trust me?

KATE. Strangely, I do.

HARRY. Madame, Dick Buckskin's my name, acting's my game. Your uncle, Colonel Thunder, incensed by Harry's expulsion from West Point, has decided to disinherit Harry and what's more has hired me, Dick Buckskin — thespian — to impersonate the real Harry so that you would fall in love with me, not he, thus barring Harry from your heart and home.

KATE. Harry from my heart and home?

HARRY. That's it in a nutshell.

KATE. Do you know my cousin Harry?

HARRY. Intimately. I'd be lost without him. Consequently, I've forewarned Harry and he intends to treat the real Colonel Thunder as an imposter.

KATE. And yet — call it woman's intuition — somehow *you* — Dick Buckskin, thespian — remind me of my cousin Harry.

HARRY. Oh, I haven't time to explain. (*He stamps three times. Rover pops up.*)

ROVER. Hi Kate!

KATE. Hi, Harry! . . . Harry!!! (*Rover ducks down again.*)

THUNDER. (*Offstage.*) Harry! Where in thunder are you?

HARRY. Quick, he's here — pretend you don't know me.

KATE. That shouldn't be hard. (*Thunder enters, buoyant.*)

THUNDER. There you two love birds are! Cut her out of the main column did ya — aimin' to rope her and put your brand on her, eh boy?

KATE. Uncle, who is this?

THUNDER. Who is this — ha! ha! ha! That's a good one! And you two out in the garden, billin' and cooin'.

HARRY. Who are you, sir?

THUNDER. Charming lad. Charming lad. Sometimes he play-acts.

KATE. So I've heard.

THUNDER. Here, niece, take from a father's hand — Harry Thunder.

41

KATE. That I cannot do.

THUNDER. Why not? (*Harry stamps three times. Rover enters. Kate takes his hand.*)

KATE. Because here, Uncle, take from my hand Harry Thunder.

THUNDER. Huh?

ROVER. Father!

THUNDER. Father! This is no son of mine!

KATE. You mean you don't recognize your own son?

THUNDER. Yes! And this ain't him!

ROVER. Father! Pappy! Da-da!

HARRY. You're overdoing it, Jack.

THUNDER. Who is this? Some puppy unknown. *This* is my son.

HARRY. I've never seen this man before in my life.

THUNDER. What!!

ROVER. Not to have a father recognize you. To have a father deny your existence. It cracks my very heart.

THUNDER. I'm going to crack your very skull in a minute. This is my son! And what the hell are you wearing? You look like a hummingbird in heat.

ROVER. The old fart's not too bad. Hey, he's got a very realistic gut on him.

THUNDER. Gut! What gut?

ROVER. He came padded for the part!

THUNDER. I've half a mind to thrash you in front of your fiancee.

KATE. Fiancee? I hardly know this man.

THUNDER. But Crow saw you sparkin' in the garden with my son.

KATE. Yes, and here he is.

THUNDER. No! And there he ain't.

KATE. It's a fickle father that forgets a son.

ROVER. For shame, father.

THUNDER. Father! I made some mistakes in my time, but you weren't one of them.

KATE. (*To Thunder, pointing to Rover.*) You don't know this man?

THUNDER. Some puppy unknown.

KATE. (*To Rover about Thunder.*) And do you know this man?

ROVER. Some hambone unknown.

THUNDER. Hambone!

KATE. Father and son are determined not to know each other.

ROVER. Oh, Kate, this man's an actor! And so am I. And so is he. And so, and so . . . "Salutation and greeting to you all, trip, trip apace good Audrey." (*Jane runs in, trips, takes Harry's arm. They dance around, much to Thunder's disapproval.*)

HARRY. "A homely thing, sir, but she's mine own."

ROVER. *As You Like It.*

THUNDER. I don't like it at all. You've not gone and married this slut?

JANE. "I thank God for my sluttishness!"

THUNDER. My son a college drop-out and now he marries a slut. (*Aside.*) Do you folks ever have these kind of days?

HARRY. And if I had gotten married, would you not support my choice?

JANE. I would!

THUNDER. Indeed I would not!

HARRY. But she's so cute! So unspoiled! So imaginatively dressed!

JANE. Well, look at yourself!

HARRY. At last, someone in this house with taste!

KATE. Uncle, I think this has gone far enough. It's time for you to recognize your only son.

ROVER. Never mind. The old boy's a good actor. I'll cast him as Charles the Wrestler in *As You Like It.* I'll trip up his heels.

THUNDER. Who'll trip up whose heels, puppy unknown! (*Thunder lifts his cane to strike Rover. Crow enters and receives the blow.*)

CROW. Ah, Colonel darlin', I'd know that blow anywhere. Mr. Buckskin, I'd like a word with you in private.

THUNDER. Buckskin?!

ROVER. Avant! (*Enter Kliegle and Leako.*)

KLIEGLE. "Light! Light! Let there be light!"

LEAKO. "Shine out fair sun till I have bought a glass."

HARRY. "All the world's a stage!"

ROVER. "Mad world! Mad kings, mad composition!"

THUNDER. You said it! Now if'n you're a real man and want to even up the score, meet me on the road south of town in an hour.

ROVER. I'll be there!

CROW. (*To Thunder.*) But we're going to be on the road *north* of town.

THUNDER. Idiot! Don't you think I know that. Chaaaarge!!! (*They exit.*)

HARRY. Don't take him seriously Jack—I mean, Harry!

ROVER. Ha-ha-ha. I don't take it seriously. A fig. A bagetelle. (*Aside.*) I mean to be on that roadside in an hour and beat the hell out of him. My wrath! Oh, my wrath!

KATE. Oh, my Harry! (*He exits. She follows.*)

JANE. "I thank God for my sluttishness!"

HARRY. I think we all do, Jane. I think we all do.

BLACKOUT

Scene 3

Kate Thunder's house.
Kate and Morales enter.
Kate is in quite a state.

KATE. I won't stand for it!

MORALES. I humbly beg your pardon, Senorita, but because I could not pay my humble rent on my humble little cassa, Ephraim Smooth has thrown me in the clutches of the not-so-humble Rancher Gammon. (*Villain music.*) Myself, I could bear it, but not my innocent, humble sister.

KATE. Ask her to come in. I've just about had it with Smooth interfering in my affairs.

MORALES. (*Calling offstage.*) Amelia! (*Amelia enters.*) Senorita, my sister. (*Morales bows and exits.*)

KATE. C'mon in honey. I feel like we got a lot to talk about.

AMELIA. Senorita!

KATE. How can I help you?

AMELIA. I had a husband, and a son . . . once. Yes once, I too knew happiness.

KATE. Are they dead?

AMELIA. Dead to me.

KATE. Would you like to talk about it?

AMELIA. Twenty years ago, when the world was young and I

was coming to the age of love, I awoke one morning to find a joy in my life. A joy which came in the shape of a man, a young man, a handsome man.

KATE. What manner of man was he?

AMELIA. A captain, in the cavalry.

KATE. An officer?

AMELIA. We were to be married in the spring.

KATE. How wonderful. Did you have a white wedding gown?

AMELIA. (*Nearly weeping.*) Yes, it was beautiful. Silken taffeta with a long train and a mantilla of lace with orange blossoms.

KATE. (*Nearly weeping.*) Ohhhhhhh!

AMELIA. (*Weeping.*) It was my mother's!

KATE. (*Weeping.*) Ohhhhhhh!

AMELIA. Then . . . fate intervened! (*They both cry. Then cease.*)

KATE. Dang! Why does Fate always have to intervene? What happened?

AMELIA. An old honest soldier—an old Indian scout—with an old Irish accent—came to my brother and myself to inform us that my beloved captain did not intend to marry me!

KATE. What?

AMELIA. He intended to hire a counterfeit clergyman to perform the service.

KATE. No!

AMELIA. But as fate would have it—

KATE. Yes?

AMELIA. The Indian scout was a born romantic with a brother who *was* a clergyman who performed the marriage.

KATE. Then you were legally married.

AMELIA. Oh, yes, it was a beautiful service.

KATE. Oh, I'm so glad.

AMELIA. Unfortunately, the marriage didn't work out. He abandoned me the next day.

KATE. Was the marriage . . . consummated?

AMELIA. Several times. Enough, at any rate, to bear fruit.

KATE. You were with child!

AMELIA. I was with child all over the Southwest. I followed fort to fort. Fort Apache. Fort Commanche. Fort after fort on foot. The Indians had a name for me—"She-who-follows-fort-after-fort-on-foot." I never found him. Distracted, I had the child and continued to follow in his fort-steps. For two years I searched in vain. Finally, when I returned half mad from grief, I learnt the couple with whom I had left the child had moved East, leaving no word, no address, no hope. Shattered, I returned to Muleshoe and was taken in by my brother, who, wounded with remorse for being the cause of my misfortune, retired from the clergy and began to grow cactus.

KATE. That's the saddest story I've ever heard. Come with me, honey, I want you and your brother to accept the hospitality of my house.

AMELIA. I'm so grateful. Oh madame, to have those two cruel hearts against us. Gammon and Smooth.

KATE. Never you mind, Amelia. You go on in now. I'll figure out some way to repay Gammon and Smooth. (*Amelia exits.*) Gammon—that bushwhacker! What's he going to pull next? (*Gammon and the three deserters barge into the room.*)

GAMMON. There she is boys, grab her!

KATE. Ask a silly question! (*They chase her around the room. She fights them off and turns to Gammon, who draws his gun.*) What do you intend to do with me, Gammon?

GAMMON. I'm gettin' rid of you lady! You and your high-minded ways! Then I'm gonna buy up the debts of all them piddley-ass farmers you been rentin' to, kick 'em off their land, and take over the territory! Get her, boys! (*They do.*)

KATE. You'll never get away with this, Gammon.

GAMMON. Oh yeah? Who's gonna stop me?

KATE. My cousin, Harry!

GAMMON. Oh yeah?

KATE. Yeah!

GAMMON. Well, for your information, girlie, he was seen leaving town today.

KATE. Oh yeah?

GAMMON. Yeah!

KATE. Oh yeah?

GAMMON. Yeah!

KATE. Whoops!

GAMMON. What've ya got to say now, girlie?

KATE. . . . HELP!!!

GAMMON. (*Aside.*) Never mind booing me. It won't bother me a bit. (*The piano player plays villain exiting music, Gammon laughs, and slinks off.*)

In the middle of nowhere. Three cactus. A railroad line. Three deserters. A damsel (Kate) tied to the tracks.

KATE. (*Gagged.*) Mnnggrrmph.
ANGEL EYES. What'd she say?
WILSON. Mnnggrrmph.
LIBERTY. The noon-day train should be along any minute now.
KATE. Mnnggrrmph.
ANGEL EYES. Why'd Gammon want us to bushwhack this here lady?
LIBERTY. So he can take over her holdings and become the richest man in the territory.
ANGEL EYES. What's in it for us?
LIBERTY. We get to bushwhack him, and *we* become the richest men in the territory!
WILSON. Someone's coming!
LIBERTY. Hide! (*All hide behind the cactus. Rover enters. He doesn't see Kate.*)
ROVER. I've decided against fighting the "Colonel." Just leave town, leave Kate safe and happy behind me.
KATE. Mnnggrrmph!
ROVER. What's that? Muffled cries?
KATE. Mnnggrrmph!!
ROVER. No. Just desert wind. (*Train whistle in the distance.*) Hmm. Noon-day train.
KATE. MNNGGRRMPH!!!*%%^^
ROVER. Strange the tricks the desert wind will play on a man. (*Colonel Thunder and Crow enter. Crow, significantly, carries a bow and arrow.*)
THUNDER. Dang me for diddlin'. Now I guess I have to fight him. (*To Rover.*) Puppy unknown—I have a quarrel to settle with you.
ROVER. Well, if it isn't the "Colonel."
THUNDER. You bet your life it's the Colonel.
ROVER. No, you're betting *your* life.
CROW. Colonel darlin', think better of this. The man's twenty years your junior.

THUNDER. I'll go easy on him. I just intend to wing the whipper-snapper. (*Rover draws his gun, twirls it ostentatiously, returns it to his holster.*) Nobody likes a show-off. Crow, you shall be my second.

CROW. All right, stand here, back to back. (*They do so.*) You're to take ten paces, turn, and fire. (*The two men, back to back. We hear in the distance a train whistle and the chugga-chugga of the engine getting closer and closer.*)

ROVER. It's not too late for you to admit you're not Colonel Thunder.

THUNDER. It's not too late for you to admit you're not my son.

CROW. One-Two-Three-Four-Five-Six-Seven-Eight-Nine — (*As they turn to draw they see Kate.*)

ROVER. Kate!

THUNDER. Niece o'mine!

ROVER. Jack Rover to the rescue! (*They run to untie her, the train approaches. As they untie her, the deserters come out from the cactus.*)

LIBERTY. Turn and draw!

THUNDER. Help! Puppy unknown!! (*Rover wheels, fires, shoots the guns out of Wilson's and Angel Eyes' hands. Liberty and Rover fistfight as the train gets closer and closer. They fight around Kate, preventing Thunder and Crow from untying her. Finally, in the nick of time, Rover punches out Liberty, stops the train, and unties Kate.*)

ROVER. Kate!

KATE. Harry!

LIBERTY. Let's go, boys! (*The deserters flee.*)

ROVER. Rascals, remain! (*Rover gives chase.*)

THUNDER. Varmits, vamoose!

KATE. Cousin, come back!

CROW. Crow to the rescue! (*Crow shoots an arrow. Offstage we hear an "Owwwww!!"*) Begorra, I hit one of them!

THUNDER. Puppy unknown!

KATE. Cousin! Come back! (*They exit, with Crow drawing another arrow. Simultaneously, Rover staggers on with three arrows in him.*)

ROVER. Fortunately, they're just flesh wounds. Duels, desperadoes, Indians . . . what next? (*A bear chases Rover offstage, doing a little dance* c. *before giving chase.*)

Outside Morales' adobe. From the adobe come Sim, Gammon and Morales. Sim is writing and crying.

GAMMON. Nothing I love more than throwing the destitute into the street. Guess I'm just a natural-born landlord. (*To Sim.*) Make sure you itemize it all, boy!

MORALES. But Senor, why do you wish to confiscate all our humble furniture?

GAMMON. I know you been complaining up to the big house — even getting Kate Thunder to intervene for you, but she can't help you now. (*To Sim.*) Quit your crying, boy, your tears are makin' the ink run.

SIM. Father, please don't be so cruel to Mr. Morales.

GAMMON. Ah, hush up! Now get back in there with the Sheriff and itemize every stick of furniture. That which we don't want, we might could use for kindlin'. (*Gammon exits.*)

SIM. Senor Morales, I wanted to help you in your hour of need. Here's my life savings — $1.23.

MORALES. Not much of a savings.

SIM. Not much of a life. (*They exit into the adobe. Enter Amelia.*)

AMELIA. Oh, I hope my brother is all right! The sudden departure of young Harry Thunder has thrown Miss Katherine into such a state of confusion as she has quite overlooked our plight! Heavens, who's this?! (*She removes herself to the side of the adobe. Enter Rover, his dress and hair disorderly, bandages all over his body.*)

ROVER. (*A puffin' and a pantin'.*) What a night. Battling desperadoes. Getting shot in the back by Indians and pursued by a bear. How many of you folks have ever been pursued by a bear? Well, I'm here to tell ya, it was an un-bearable ex-perience. (*Sensing the audience's hostility.*) Okay, okay. Just a little joke. He chased me for miles, folks! Chased me all night! Chased me into a box canyon. There I was trapped like a rat. The bear advanced. I could feel his hot bear breath breathing on me. Nothing more disgusting than hot bear breath. There I was. A goner. He reared up on his hind legs about to pounce. There was nothing left to do — so — I began to recite Shakespeare.

At first the bear seemed curious. Puzzled, then pleased, then actually moved. I believe I saw the beast shed a tear. Unfortunately, then I came to the line "Like to a chaos or an unlicked bear whelp." I think the bear took it personally. I know it wasn't my line reading. Anyway, the chase was on once more until as you just saw I outran him and escaped, but just barely. Thus ends a grizzly tale. (*He slumps against the rock.*)

AMELIA. (*Advancing.*) Sir, are you not well?

ROVER. Well, I'm better now.

AMELIA. You have been in a fight.

ROVER. More like three fights. Bandits, Indians and a bear.

AMELIA. Oh, my. Would you like some water?

ROVER. I surely would, ma'am.

AMELIA. Why, you're as weak as a lamb. (*She holds the ladle to his lips. He drinks.*) There you are, my son.

ROVER. Son? Why did you call me that? No one's ever called me that before.

AMELIA. Oh, just that I'm a sentimental old fool. When I see a young man like you, I think of the young son I never had.

ROVER. We are alike in that, for I grew up motherless. Ah, your hand feels cool upon my brow, mother.

AMELIA. Now it is I that am the embarrassed one, to hear a young man call me mother.

ROVER. Well, this is how it is. I used to make my living providing people with entertaining illusions to make them forget their loneliness for an hour or so. What's one more false characterization? (*Pause. Light change.*)

AMELIA. The sun sets. The cricket chirps.

ROVER. I feel a strange contentment come over me — as if I'd been a long way a-strayin'. (*Suddenly a disturbance from the adobe. The Sheriff carrying a chair emerges, followed by Sim and Morales.*)

MORALES. Stop! Stop!

SIM. Stop! Thief!

SHERIFF. I'm no thief. I'm a duly licensed official carrying out his official duty!

AMELIA. But that's my favorite chair. It was my mother's chair!

SHERIFF. It's my duty, ma'am.

ROVER. Then, scoundrel, know a man's first duty is

50

tenderness and civility to a woman.

SHERIFF. I'm the Sheriff here, representing Mr. Gammon.

ROVER. More's the shame then. Every officer should be a gentleman, and when he represents a low life like Gammon he shames the badge. Tell me, Sheriff, have you ever been astonished?

SHERIFF. How's that?

ROVER. Because, sir, I wish to astonish you. (*Rover stikes the Sheriff.*) Now sir, you are astonished.

SHERIFF. Just for that, I'll bring an action suit against you!

ROVER. Right! "Suit the action to the word and the word to the action." (*Rover strikes him again.*) See there, you are astonished a second time. Now I shall amaze you!!

SHERIFF. (*Dropping the chair.*) No! I'm as amazed and astonished as I want to get!

ROVER. Then get! (*Rover stamps his foot. The Sheriff scurries away.*) Your chair, madame.

AMELIA. Oh, thank you. (*She sits. He kisses her hand.*)

ROVER. Your obedient servant, madame. (*Jane enters.*)

JANE. Mister Thunder, you must haste and fly.

ROVER. Why? Why must I haste and fly?

JANE. Because they're rounding up a posse to hang you.

ROVER. You're right. I must haste and fly. We shall meet again if there's a God in Heaven. (*Thunder.*) We shall meet again.

AMELIA. What posse? Who's behind all this?

JANE. My father and Smooth. They think he's one of those bandits they've posted a reward for. They're gonna take him to the saloon and hang him.

MORALES. This is Senor Gammon's way of getting revenge on Senor Thunder for taking my side in our quarrel.

AMELIA. I'll speak to Miss Katherine. He shall have justice. As he defended me, so shall I—Amelia Dolores Morales—defend him. Brother, come. Hell hath no fury like a woman scorned.

JANE. Have you been scorned?

AMELIA. Honey, you don't know the half of it. Vamonos! (*They all exit.*)

SCENE 6

The Last Chance Saloon. Night. Jane alone.

JANE. An empty saloon is a dreary place without the sight of a lot of drunken, disgusting men. Everyone's out looking for Miss Kate's cousin Harry. It'll certainly break her heart if anything happens to him. His going, however, spoils all our fine play, and I was just beginning to learn my lines. (*She looks at her image in the mirror. Ephraim enters unseen*).

EPHRAIM. A damsel in need of healing . . . Hallelujah! (*He sneaks up on her.*)

JANE. Folks say that when you look in a mirror at night you can see the devil. (*She sees Ephraim over her shoulder. She lets out a shriek.*)

EPHRAIM. Why child, did I frighten you?

JANE. No, I always shriek this time of night.

EPHRAIM. I fear for your soul, my child.

JANE. My soul?!

EPHRAIM. You have been contaminated by these players. I must remedy that.

JANE. Indeed, and what is your remedy?

EPHRAIM. Why, you must embrace God, my child.

JANE. God? Or a man of God?

EPHRAIM. (*Coming closer.*) It is natural for woman to love man. And through loving come closer to heaven. God is the sun and thou the honeysuckle.

JANE. And thou?

EPHRAIM. I am the bee that must sting thee. Hallelujah! (*He lunges at her — misses.*) You can't elude me for long. It's a very small room and they've removed most of the furniture. (*He lunges at her again. She hits him with a large vase.*) You know, Jane, sometimes I get the feeling you don't like me. (*Kate enters, unseen by Smooth. Kate sizes up the situation, and exchanges a glance with Jane.*)

JANE. (*Aside.*) Now's my chance to show Miss Kate what a cactus-pear this Smooth really is.

EPHRAIM. Will you avoid clasping me to your breast, Jane, and thus risk damnation?

JANE. Then must I yield?

EPHRAIM. Then must you yield, lady.

JANE. Then I must be wooed like a lady. Like a fine, rich lady.

EPHRAIM. Like a fine, rich lady them, for that is what I offer if you'll be mine.

JANE. How's that?

EPHRAIM. The Church of Christian Suffering and Denial is soon to come into a great sum of money.

JANE. Now you must kneel. (*He kneels.*)

EPHRAIM. Yes, my lady, yes.

JANE. And now my foot, Ephraim.

EPHRAIM. (*Grovelling.*) Oh Jane, I knew you understood me. (*He kisses her foot repeatedly. Kate moves behind Ephraim.*)

JANE. So you intend to steal Miss Thunder's estate.

EPHRAIM. Let's call it a donation. I yearn.

JANE. Soon you will learn.

EPHRAIM. I burn.

JANE. True, you are soon to be burnt.

EPHRAIM. When will we be one?

JANE. You are undone! (*Kate taps Ephraim from behind.*)

EPHRAIM. Aaaaaahhhh!!!!

KATE. Ephraim, for weeks now I been wanting to tell you what I really think of you but now I can't because I'm a lady. I can't. I can't. The hell I can't. You're a low-down, back-slidin', two-faced, double-talkin', double-crossin', side-windin', back-bitin', slimey-tongued, counterfeitin', con-coctin', irreligious, sanctimonious—(*She takes a big gasp of air.*)—deceptive, deceitful, deludin', delusive, delusory, ersatz, nickle-plated, dime-store, two-bit, greasy-eared, four-flushin', falsifyin', fabricatin' polecat and a fraud.

EPHRAIM. I am not greasy-eared.

KATE. Git!!!

EPHRAIM. Hallelujah! (*He exits rapidly.*)

KATE. Kate Thunder is herself again.

JANE. Well, here's one rascal we're well rid of. I've prepared Madame Amelia's room, Miss. Any word of your cousin Harry?

KATE. No! None! And now that I have thrown off the chains of the Church of Christian Suffering and Denial my heart yearns all the more to see him. Go, tell them to renew their search. (*Jane exits. Amelia enters.*)

AMELIA. Oh, Madame, might I implore your influence?

KATE. Amelia, honey, I'm sorry I've neglected you. My mind has been tied up with the fate of my cousin. (*Enter Crow and Thunder, Thunder being restrained by Crow.*)

THUNDER. Damn you, Crow, we should've helped puppy unknown.

CROW. What could we do? There were three of them and only three of us.

THUNDER. He probably died thinking me a side-windin' four-flusher.

CROW. (*Reminding Thunder of past indiscretions.*) But you *are* a side-winding, four-flusher! What about Miss Amelia? (*He sees Amelia. Aside.*) Saints preserve us, Miss Amelia! Come Colonel darlin', time we were leaving!

THUNDER. Leaving? We just got here. Get your hands off me, you mangy, good for nothin'—(*Thunder and Amelia see each other. Everyone freezes—then Amelia faints. Kate and Crow help her to a chair. Thunder, simply.*) Amelia . . . it's my Amelia.

KATE. Do you two know each other?

AMELIA. (*Recovering.*) Oh! Seymour! (*She swoons again.*)

KATE. Poor woman's out of her head. She thinks you're someone named Seymour.

AMELIA. (*Recovering.*) Oh, Seymour! (*She swoons again.*)

KATE. Whoever this Seymour was, he must have meant a great deal to her.

AMELIA. (*Once again.*) Oh, Seymour! (*She swoons again.*)

THUNDER. I feel so low I could sit on a dime and dangle my legs. Oh niece! I've done this lady wrong. (*Amelia recovers.*) Dear Amelia, from the first month I deserted you I haven't known any peace of conscience. I heard you had gone to the great reward. Ah, Amelia, if only I'd married you all those years ago.

KATE. But you did!

THUNDER. Huh?

KATE. But you've been married honestly all these years. Some Indian scout—whom I now perceive to be you—substituted the real clergyman. In fact, his own brother. (*Morales enters.*)

CROW. Ah! And here he is now! My half-brother, Micheline!

MORALES. My half-brother, Fernando!

AMELIA. Our family, re-united at last!

CROW. And since you were a bonafide clergyman at the time,

the marriage between the Colonel and Amelia is a true one.

THUNDER. How can you be brothers? You're an Irish-Indian, you're Mexican.

MORALES. Our parents knew no prejudice.

THUNDER. But that makes you both brothers to Miss Amelia.

CROW and MORALES and AMELIA. That's correct!

THUNDER. You never told me that!

CROW. You never asked!

KATE. Amelia, I'm happy you've found your roving husband at last. But Uncle, this first marriage annuls the second and disinherits my cousin Harry.

THUNDER. Well, that's life all over, isn't it?

KATE. And what about your son?

THUNDER. A son? We had a son?

AMELIA. He's lost and gone forever.

THUNDER. It's only as much as I deserve. And yet if ever a father could choose a second son, I'd adopt no better than that brave, kind lad who saved my life — the one you insist on calling Harry. Amelia, he wouldn't let anyone shoot me but himself. I'd like to make him my heir.

AMELIA. He was going to shoot you, and you want to make him your heir?

THUNDER. Indeed I do. If not for this fellow, Amelia, you might never have found your husband, Captain Seymour, in Colonel Croftus Thunder. (*Enter Sheriff.*)

SHERIFF. Well, we done caught up the varmit responsible for all this.

THUNDER. Seein' as there ain't a judge within a hundred miles, I must assume the positions of judge, jury, and hangman and be firm and impartial, though he be my son. (*Rover enters, bound, followed by deserters, Gammon and Sim.*)

GAMMON. Good, because it is your son!

THUNDER. Puppy unknown!

KATE. Cousin, you're alive! Gammon, you polecat!

SHERIFF. This is the varmit who's been repeatedly terrorizin' the territory.

GAMMON. Smooth's done posted a reward and I'm a-claimin' it as mine. (*Ephraim bounds in.*)

EPHRAIM. Hallelujah!

KATE. Ephraim! You're a man of God! Appeal to them.

EPHRAIM. Hang him! Hang the iniquitous one! Hang him!

ALL. Hang him!

ROVER. Kate, if you have any more suggestions, keep them to yourself.

KATE. Uncle, draw your gun!

THUNDER. Yes, I—

KATE. Now we'll see—(*The deserters all draw their guns.*) That you guys are fast!

ROVER. Sweetheart, I realize you're just trying to help.

KATE. You're not going to shoot this man!

EPHRAIM. No, we're gonna hang him! Hang him!

ALL. Hang him!

KATE. You won't hang him! I swear it! I swear by the rafters over my head!

EPHRAIM. Good idea! The rafters—we'll hang him over the rafters!

ALL. Hang him over the rafters!

KATE. That wasn't such a good idea either. Was it?

ROVER. No, Kate, no it wasn't.

THUNDER. Thunderation, what you're doing is against the law!

LIBERTY. We'll show you law—Western law! (*A noose falls from over the bar. They drag Rover up on the bar, put the noose around his neck. MUZ enters and strolls up to Kate.*)

KATE. I've never seen you before. What're you doing here?

MUZ. Well, the card game broke up backstage.

KATE. No time for that now. They're hanging my cousin Harry. Run and fetch the law.

MUZ. Okay. But that's not your cousin Harry. (*Muz exits.*)

SIM. Can I do anything to help?

KATE. Follow that man! (*Sim exits the opposite direction.*)

EPHRAIM. Hang him! Hang him high!

ALL. Hang him! Hang him high!

ROVER. WAIT! Don't I even get a few last words?

KATE. Yeah! Doesn't he even get a few last words?

GAMMON. Oh well, okay.

ROVER. For a few last words I'd like to recite the entire Shakespearean canon. (*There is a moan from the group.*) "If music be the food of love, play on." (*The piano player plays* "Hearts and

Flowers.")* Oh Kate. I have never loved another but you.

KATE. Then why did you leave me?

ROVER. Oh Kate, because I am not worthy of you. Because I am a penniless player. Because I come before you bereft of friend, family, fortune.

KATE. What care I of friend, family, fortune. It's you I love.

ROVER. Oh, Kate. If I had the good Lord work a hundred years a makin' me the perfect mate I'd say no thanks Lord. I'll just take Kate.

ALL. Ohhhh....

ROVER. Oh, Kate, when we first met I loved you because you were like a girl from a finishing school.

KATE. I went to one. They just couldn't finish me, that's all.

ROVER. But then we rehearsed *Taming of the Shrew*. And I realized what I had suspected all along.

KATE. Which was?

ROVER. Under all that satin and lace?

KATE. Yes?

ROVER. Was a real woman!

KATE. That's what I was waiting to hear you say! Pardner! (*She produces a bullwhip from beneath her skirts, and, disarming everyone, herds them into a corner. Rover turns around and she snaps the ropes behind his back, then the noose around his neck.*)

ROVER. I love a woman with a whip! (*Rover jumps off the bar and is wound up by Kate in her whip. Muz returns with the Marshal.*)

MUZ. The Marshal has just returned from Medicine Wells. He understands the whole thing, cause he was sittin' out front the whole time!

MARSHAL. What have you varmits got to say for yourselves?

ALL. I'll never do it again!

MARSHAL. Sorry about this ma'am. Glad to be part of this happy gathering. Let's go.

EPHRAIM. Hallelujah brothers. Join me in song! (*They all exit. Ephraim leads them in* "Yes We'll Gather at the River." *Harry and Jane enter, hand in hand.*)

HARRY. Stop everybody! Jane and I have something to tell you all. (*Thunder embraces Rover.*)

AMELIA. Then Seymour, you know him too?

*See Special Note on copyright page.

57

THUNDER. Know him? He saved my life.

ROVER. Oh, so they think you're the Colonel and she thinks you're someone named Seymour. You really are a fine actor!

HARRY. Stop everybody! Jane and I have something to tell you all.

KATE. Oh uncle, be reconciled with him.

THUNDER. Reconciled? If I should not be reconciled with him I should be unworthy of the life he rescued. But sir, who are you?

HARRY. I say, stop everybody, Jane and I have something to tell you all.

THUNDER. But first, who are you puppy unknown?

ROVER. My name is Jack Rover. (*Everyone in the room quivers as if a mild electrical shock had passed through them.*)

HARRY. Stop everybody! Jane and I have something to tell you all.

ROVER. Yes, it is time for all masks to be lowered. I am not the son of Colonel Croftus Thunder. (*Everyone takes front.*) There. The truth. I've said it. And now I must leave you all.

KATE. Cousin . . .

ROVER. And I'm not your cousin! I'm an actor. And so is this man. And this old hambone as well.

THUNDER. Hambone!

HARRY. Jack, I might as well tell you that I, Dick Buckskin, thespian, am in reality, Harry Thunder. (*Everyone takes* U.) Well, I am.

ROVER. Sure you are. And this old tub of lard I suppose is the real Colonel Thunder.

HARRY. He is.

THUNDER. I am.

ROVER. Would someone please clear all this up. (*Everyone looks around confusedly. Sim runs to Rover but is stopped by Harry's line.*)

HARRY. Stop, everybody. Jane and I have something to tell you all.

THUNDER. Tell me, puppy unknown, where do you call home?

ROVER. Home? I haven't any. I've been strolling player all my life.

THUNDER. But from whence did your strolling commence?

ROVER. Here in the West.

THUNDER. The West?

ROVER. But I was raised in the East.

THUNDER. East.

ROVER. My mother was an Army camp follower, forever on the move from one fort to another.

KATE. (*Aside to Amelia.*) Did you hear that?

AMELIA. Why do you think I'm wearing this blissful expression?

ROVER. Thru extremities of circumstances, I was separated from my mother.

AMELIA. Can you remember the name of the town where you were separated?

ROVER. Bent Fork.

AMELIA. (*Blissfully.*) Bent Fork. Not *the* Bent Fork?

ROVER. Yes, the Bent Fork.

AMELIA. Excuse me, sir, what was the name of the lady that bore you.

ROVER. My mother's name was Seymour.

THUNDER. Why Amelia . . .

AMELIA. My son!

ROVER. Ma?

AMELIA. It is my Seymour! (*They embrace.*)

THUNDER. Seymour? You named him Seymour Seymour?

AMELIA. Son—your father!

ROVER. Can it be? Heavens, then I have attempted to raise a hand against a father's life.

THUNDER. Thunderation! The puppy unknown defends a father without knowing it. I gain a son.

AMELIA. And I a son!

MORALES. And I a nephew!

HARRY. And I a brother!

KATE. And I a cousin!

SIM. And I a . . .

KATE. And a husband, I hope.

ROVER. Oh, yes.

JANE. So you're *not* Dick Buckskin?

HARRY. No, I'm Harry Thunder.

KATE. And you're not Harry Thunder?

ROVER. No, I'm Jack Rover.

AMELIA. No, you're Seymour Seymour.

ROVER. Seymour Seymour — it's a hell of a name, Ma.

THUNDER. Harry, you've lost your fortune to an elder brother.

HARRY. Yes, but before I had a brother I had a friend — Jack Rover. A friend I prized above all others. Above all fortunes. And now my cousin Kate gains a fortune in my friend. And I'd like to take this opportunity to tell you all that Jane and I have something to tell you all.

MUZ. You mean?

HARRY. Yes.

ALL. You mean?

HARRY. Yes. Jane and I are to be married.

MUZ. (*Sentimentally.*) Oh, it was worth coming back to the play to see this touching scene.

AMELIA. (*To Kate.*) So you are willing to take our Seymour?

KATE. Seymour, Jack Rover, Harry Thunder — what's in a name? But you must know — I've renounced my religion and therefore my fortune — it is I who comes penniless before you.

ROVER. You loved me when I had nothing. Nothing in the world could make me love you less.

KATE. Then you'll have me?

ROVER. With or without your fortune, as you will.

THUNDER. Then it shall be *with* your fortune. As Loftus's next living relative after his daughter, I inherit all that was his, which I promptly give back to you again.

KATE. Gratefully I accept both my fortune and your son, on the condition that your fortune that should go to your son whom I know as Harry, should go to your son whom *you* know as Harry.

HARRY. I'm so glad *you* said that!

KATE. Oh Harry, I mean Jack, I mean Seymour. My roving boy.

ROVER. Oh Kate — "The prettiest Kate in Christendom." I'll go no more a roving. I've sown the last of my wild oats. (*Everyone goes "Ahhh..." as they embrace. There is a big explosion off-stage. Kliegle and Leako enter with lit lights. The prisoners and Marshal follow.*)

KLIEGLE. Phosphorescent, Mr. Leako.

LEAKO. Candlelabrum, Mr. Kliegle.

ROVER. "Angelic Creature."
KATE. You're not so bad yourself.
ROVER. "Angelic creature."
KATE. Oh, go on.
ROVER. Kate, I'm trying to do the epilogue.
KATE. Well who's stopping you?
ROVER. "Angelic creature." Friends, family, all. A spark from Shakespeare was my muse, the star that led me through the maze of life and brought me at last to heart and home. "To merit friends so good, so sweet wife, the tender husband by my part of life. My wild oats sown, let candid thespian law decree that glorious harvest—your applause."

PROPERTY LIST

ACT ONE

Scene 1
Piano
Bar, with bottles & glasses
Cash box
Sabre (Thunder)
Tomahawk (Crow)

Scene 2
Luggage

Scene 3
Wheelbarrow
Suitcase
Buckets of water
Purse, with money (Rover)

Scene 4
Handkerchief (Rover)
Lighting instruments

Scene 5
Account books, pens etc.
Skull
Purse (Kate)

Scene 6
Hotel register
Pistols (3)

ACT TWO

Scene 1
Pistols (3)

Scene 2
Folding screen
Cane (Thunder)

Scene 3
Pistol (Gammon)

Scene 4
Cacti (3)
Railroad tracks
Rope
Bow & arrow (Crow)
Pistols (4)

Scene 5
Pad & pen
Water ladle
Chair

Scene 6
Large vase
Rope
Bullwhip (Kate)
Lighting instruments

NEW PLAYS

★ **SHEL'S SHORTS by Shel Silverstein.** Lauded poet, songwriter and author of children's books, the incomparable Shel Silverstein's short plays are deeply infused with the same wicked sense of humor that made him famous. "…[a] childlike honesty and twisted sense of humor." *–Boston Herald.* "…terse dialogue and an absurdity laced with a tang of dread give [*Shel's Shorts*] more than a trace of Samuel Beckett's comic existentialism." *–Boston Phoenix.* [flexible casting] ISBN: 0-8222-1897-6

★ **AN ADULT EVENING OF SHEL SILVERSTEIN by Shel Silverstein.** Welcome to the darkly comic world of Shel Silverstein, a world where nothing is as it seems and where the most innocent conversation can turn menacing in an instant. These ten imaginative plays vary widely in content, but the style is unmistakable. "…[*An Adult Evening*] shows off Silverstein's virtuosic gift for wordplay…[and] sends the audience out…with a clear appreciation of human nature as perverse and laughable." *–NY Times.* [flexible casting] ISBN: 0-8222-1873-9

★ **WHERE'S MY MONEY? by John Patrick Shanley.** A caustic and sardonic vivisection of the institution of marriage, laced with the author's inimitable razor-sharp wit. "…Shanley's gift for acid-laced one-liners and emotionally tumescent exchanges is certainly potent…" *–Variety.* "…lively, smart, occasionally scary and rich in reverse wisdom." *–NY Times.* [3M, 3W] ISBN: 0-8222-1865-8

★ **A FEW STOUT INDIVIDUALS by John Guare.** A wonderfully screwy comedy-drama that figures Ulysses S. Grant in the throes of writing his memoirs, surrounded by a cast of fantastical characters, including the Emperor and Empress of Japan, the opera star Adelina Patti and Mark Twain. "Guare's smarts, passion and creativity skyrocket to awesome heights…" *–Star Ledger.* "…precisely the kind of good new play that you might call an everyday miracle…every minute of it is fresh and newly alive…" *–Village Voice.* [10M, 3W] ISBN: 0-8222-1907-7

★ **BREATH, BOOM by Kia Corthron.** A look at fourteen years in the life of Prix, a Bronx native, from her ruthless girl-gang leadership at sixteen through her coming to maturity at thirty. "…vivid world, believable and eye-opening, a place worthy of a dramatic visit, where no one would want to live but many have to." *–NY Times.* "…rich with humor, terse vernacular strength and gritty detail…" *–Variety.* [1M, 9W] ISBN: 0-8222-1849-6

★ **THE LATE HENRY MOSS by Sam Shepard.** Two antagonistic brothers, Ray and Earl, are brought together after their father, Henry Moss, is found dead in his seedy New Mexico home in this classic Shepard tale. "…His singular gift has been for building mysteries out of the ordinary ingredients of American family life…" *–NY Times.* "…rich moments …Shepard finds gold." *–LA Times.* [7M, 1W] ISBN: 0-8222-1858-5

★ **THE CARPETBAGGER'S CHILDREN by Horton Foote.** One family's history spanning from the Civil War to WWII is recounted by three sisters in evocative, intertwining monologues. "…bittersweet music—[a] rhapsody of ambivalence…in its modest, garrulous way…theatrically daring." *–The New Yorker.* [3W] ISBN: 0-8222-1843-7

★ **THE NINA VARIATIONS by Steven Dietz.** In this funny, fierce and heartbreaking homage to *The Seagull*, Dietz puts Chekhov's star-crossed lovers in a room and doesn't let them out. "A perfect little jewel of a play…" *–Shepherdstown Chronicle.* "…a delightful revelation of a writer at play; and also an odd, haunting, moving theater piece of lingering beauty." *–Eastside Journal (Seattle).* [1M, 1W (flexible casting)] ISBN: 0-8222-1891-7

DRAMATISTS PLAY SERVICE, INC.
440 Park Avenue South, New York, NY 10016 212-683-8960 Fax 212-213-1539
postmaster@dramatists.com www.dramatists.com